You Mu

You Must be Joking

POPULAR EXCUSES FOR AVOIDING JESUS CHRIST

by

MICHAEL GREEN

HODDER AND STOUGHTON
LONDON SYDNEY AUCKLAND TORONTO

ACKNOWLEDGMENTS

The author and publishers wish to acknowledge copyright material from:

Quintessence, Blue Mountain Music, 155–157 Oxford Street, London W1

Dave Crosby, Warner Bros. Music Ltd., 69 New Oxford Street, London W1

Gordon Bailey, SOL Publications, Box 356, Birmingham

Roger McGough, © Roger McGough, 1967 Penguin Modern Poets 10, Corgi Publications, Century House, 61–63 Uxbridge Road, London W5

M. B. Yeats, Miss Anne Yeats and the Macmillan Company of London and Basingstoke for a quotation from 'Death' (The Collected Poems of W. B. Yeats)

Contents

Preface

The stimulus to write this sort of book came from Friedrich Hänssler, the head of Hänssler-Verlag, publishers. The idea and title emerged as I lay in bed in Durban with meningitis under the care and imaginative friendship of Dr. John Hill. The chapter headings came from the many jokers who have tried them out on me. Valuable suggestions came from Tony Collins of Hodder and Stoughton. The typing came from my overworked secretary Anne Johnson.

TO ONE AND ALL, THANK YOU.

I

From the Author . . .

IF I HAD called this 'Foreword' or 'Preface' you would have skipped it, in all probability. But I want you to read it. It is quite important, and it shows what the book is about.

A STARTLING AGREEMENT ...

In recent years I have had the opportunity of travelling widely in Europe, Asia, Africa, North America and Australia. I have had the chance to discover the basic attitudes to life adopted by ordinary people of every conceivable variety of background, colour and education. You would expect these attitudes to differ enormously; and on most subjects, of course, they do. But on one subject there is startling agreement. When it is a matter of what men think about human nature and religion, man's origin and destiny, the possibility of forgiveness or life after death — then people tend to come up with the same answers, whether they hail from Paramatta or Portsmouth. Such agreement looks at first sight, to be very encouraging: when the United Nations can rarely agree about anything at all, it is amazing that men all over the world should tend to think alike about the basic questions of our existence. However, I am not very impressed by this apparent unanimity.

... BUT SHALLOW

For one thing it is shallow. When you broach the question of religion, and a fellow replies 'Oh, but all religions lead to God', ten to one he knows almost nothing about his own religious background, still less about any other. When he says, 'I'm not the religious sort', you can be fairly confident that he has made no investigation whatever into whether or not there is a religious sort, and, if there is, what it is like. When he says, 'Jesus was just a marvellous teacher but no more', it is unusual to find that he has ever examined the claims Jesus made, or the evidence supporting those claims. When you hear a person say, 'I do my best — no man can do more', of one thing you can be certain: he does not do his best (which of us does?) but he hasn't the honesty to admit as much. So do you see why I am not all that impressed by these parrot cries which come up, as regular as clockwork, whenever I begin to talk about God? They are so shallow. They simply show that people, on the whole, are content not to *think* about the really important matters of life and death. 'Oh, I have no time for religion,' says a prosperous business man who spends an hour a day keeping up with the Stock Market. But if there is a God, if there is a heaven, if there is forgiveness, what an appallingly short-sighted attitude! The man who invests shrewdly and carefully in his stocks and shares may be pathetically naïve and incompetent when it comes to investing in life.

. . . AND ESCAPIST

There's another reason why I am not impressed by the common responses about religion which I meet everywhere I go. They are not only shallow, betraying an absence of thought: they are also evasive, betraying an unwillingness to face up to the evidence. Many of the things people come out with, when you ask them their fundamental attitudes to life, boil down to something like the answers I examine in the chapters which follow. And the trouble is that they are not only shallow but dishonest. The man who says, 'It doesn't matter what you believe so long as you are sincere', would never dream of applying that motto to any area of life other than religion. He may think he's being straightforward when he comes out with a statement like this, but he isn't really. What he means is that he is not going to take the trouble to investigate the truth of Christianity or of any other religion — maybe because he doesn't think it important enough, maybe because he fears he would get exposed, or challenged, or involved. Although he sounds so fine and liberal-minded, he is likely to be an escapist at heart.

You see, then, why I am not satisfied to find such widespread agreement about fundamental beliefs? The agreement is unthinking and escapist. It is an agnosticism which does not want to know in case the answer should prove costly or inconvenient. So right at the outset of this little book, I am going to ask you to be different.

A PLEA FOR HONESTY

Will you stand out from the crowd, and think for yourself? Will you have the courage to examine the evidence and ask yourself how sound are the assumptions about God and meaning, life and death, with which you have lived so far? Will they bear the weight of your life and future? After all, these *are* the basic issues. It makes an enormous difference if there is a God or not; if he has revealed himself or not; if he will accept us or not; whether we have a future after death or not. It simply will not do to hide our heads in the sand, repeat our parrot cries, and refuse to see how they stand up to critical examination. The Old Testament has some trenchant things to say about people 'who make lies their refuge; and the rain shall sweep away the refuge of lies' (Isaiah 28:15, 17). Could your refuge be like that? A famous insurance company has as one of its selling gimmicks the picture of a roof, and the phrase 'Refuge for Life'. Well, have you got a roof that will keep the rain out? The New Testament (Matthew 7:24f) records the contrast between the man who built the house of his life on the rock and the one who built on sand: the rain and the wind and the floods assail both houses, but only the house on the rock can withstand the onslaught. Could it be that you are building on sand?

I have collected here a number of very common assumptions about the most important issues in life. You may recognise one or more of them that you share. Very well, why not begin with that chapter, and ask yourself if the assumption is well founded — or mistaken? Let me, for my part, come clean at the outset. To my mind these assumptions sound good, but they won't do. They are dangerous fallacies, and offer no proper foundation for life. Time and again when folk have brought them forward I have felt (or said!) 'You must be joking!' Will you, too, come clean at the outset? Lay aside prejudice; examine the evidence; and be prepared for change should you become persuaded that your assumptions won't hold water. These matters are of critical importance to all of us. There really is no excuse for shallow thinking or evasive action as we look into them together.

2

'I'm not the religious sort'

THE RELIGIOUS SORT

'No, VICAR, GO and talk to someone else. I'm afraid I'm not the religious sort.' That is very often said, and I have a lot of sympathy with it. There is something creepy and sanctimonious, something effeminate and wet about that phrase 'the religious sort'. I think of business men in black ties at the funeral of one of their companions trying to imitate 'the religious sort' for half an hour, and then emerging breathless from the funeral to the open air in order to light up a cigarette and return to normality. I think of a country church with six people in it along with the vicar, not to mention a bat or two, while the men of the village meet across the green in the pub for a cheerful evening in each other's company. Church? Not for them, thank you; they're not the religious sort. Or the mind strays, perhaps, to some ceremonial occasion in a great cathedral: the trumpeters, the taperers, the choir, the candles, the expensive robes, the perfectly rendered service which nobody seems to mean — all of this evokes the response, 'I'm not the religious sort'. Or take two very different examples of 'religion'. One comes on the radio with the daily service and a handful of singers who may sound professional and bogus: canned religion is not attractive at the best of times. The other comes in a great stadium where the evangelist is urging people to come to the front for counselling: that can seem a mere playing on the religious emotions — and 'I'm not the religious sort'.

HYPOCRISY?

Why do we so strongly dislike 'the religious sort'? Is it not because we have almost come to regard religion and hypocrisy as the same thing? There is a very long history of this. In Isaiah's day back in the eighth century B.C. men were offering God all manner of sacrifices, but their hearts were far from him. In Jesus' day the scribes and pharisees gained the reputation for being hypocrites. Many of them must have been absolutely genuine. Some, however, were seen to make long prayers in order to impress; to give ostentatiously so that everyone should think how generous they were; to make a great show of their biblical knowledge in order to shame others. Piety outside and corruption inside is a revolting mixture. Jesus had to accuse some of his hearers of being just like that: they reminded him of the white sepulchres which were such a common sight on the hills set against the deep blue of the Sea of Galilee. They looked marvellous from the outside: but inside they were foul and full of corruption and dead men's bones.

The link between religion and hypocrisy did not die in the first century. Think of the hypocrisy in those very religious days of the Victorian era: the immorality that flourished, the exploitation that went on alongside meticulous religious observance. And, rightly or wrongly, there are many who suspect hypocrisy in the high churchgoing figures among the whites in Rhodesia and South Africa, and among the middle class in America. Could this be a sort of insurance policy to preserve the regimes against the inroads of black power and Communism? I do not know. But what I do know is that many people assert very forcefully that they are not the religious sort because they hate hypocrisy, and they feel that somehow it is tied up with religion.

BEGGING?

Closely allied to this is begging. None of us like seeing beggars. It makes us feel uncomfortable; indeed, we feel 'got at'. But organised religion bears the image of the beggar. How many churches do you pass with a notice outside inviting you to save this ancient building? How many cathedrals do you go into with a notice inside telling you how much per minute it costs to run the place? Then there are the fêtes, the whist drives, the door to door collections, the stewardship campaigns and all the other money raising gimmicks. The churches always seem after your cash. And we are very wary of folk who are after our cash. Let's make it crystal clear that we are not the religious sort.

I take the force of all this. Indeed, that is why I said at the outset that I have a lot of sympathy with people who say they are not the religious sort. But all the same I think they are wrong.

CLEARING THE AIR

First, let me clear the air and have a look at those justifiable objections to the religious sort which have just been raised. It is true that a lot of bad things have been done in the name of religion. So they have in the name of medicine, but that does not mean we don't go near a doctor. A lot of good things have been done in the name of religion, too: but that by itself does not make it true. There is only one proper question for men of integrity: is the religious account of the world and man true? If it is, then I want it, however many bad things have sheltered under its umbrella. I shall want to throw out into the rain the bad things, but not to take down the umbrella.

It is perfectly true that some expressions of religion border on the nauseating — always remembering that what is nauseating to one man is meat and drink to another. I personally get switched off very fast indeed by B.B.C. services and cathedrals. Others get annoyed by prayer meetings, evangelistic rallies or good old Anglican Matins. I have no doubt that there is a great deal of insincerity in church circles, and I have no doubt that illicit psychological pressure is exerted by some evangelists. But once again, back to the basic facts. Did they or did they not happen? Was Jesus or was he not the Son of God? Did he, or did he not rise from the dead? If he did, then I can afford to be broadminded about types of religious expression I personally dislike. If not, then the whole lot is rubbish, a type of escapism for which I have no time at all.

As for hypocrisy and money grabbing, these need not detain us long. Just because there are counterfeit coins about, that does not stop you using money, does it? Indeed, were there no good money, nobody would bother with making counterfeit. So the existence of hypocrisy in religious circles is no reason for rejecting religion. It rather suggests that there is a genuine article as well as spurious copies. Take a good hard look at Jesus in the Gospels. There is not a sniff of hypocrisy about him. He was the first to denounce it in others. And it is with Jesus that we are concerned. Following him means following the one who denounced hypocrisy and would have no part in it at all. Just because some of his followers have failed to live up to that, it does not stop you having a go.

On the money-grabbing issue, I think the church has deserved its appalling image. It does give the impression that it is always out for money. It should rather proclaim that it has found great treasure in Jesus Christ, and that unlike most treasures, this one is for free. Jesus was always impressing upon people that entry into the Kingdom of God, or the Great Supper or friendship with himself (all three add up to the same thing) was absolutely free, for black and white, Jew and Gentile, prostitute and Pharisee alike. Free. But he also made it plain that life within the kingdom was costly. It might cost you all you have, just as it cost him all he had. So the church is right to say to its members that they owe Christ a proportion of their time as well as their money and their talents. The church is wrong to ask those who are not its committed members to act as if they were. To them the free generosity of Christ's acceptance of any man who comes to him should be the main message that gets through. If that message is not being heard, it is not because Christ has changed his attitude, but because the church is being unfaithful to his teaching and example. So if this matter of money has been bugging you, forget it. Jesus is the one we are concerned with. And he never went round taking collections from folk who dropped in for the odd funeral. He never put a collecting box outside the Nazareth synagogue begging non-members to prop it up. If the church does not follow his example, so much the worse for the church. Don't let it stop you finding the most wonderful person in the world, Jesus himself.

Having, I hope, cleared the air, I now want to ask some pertinent questions of any who are hiding behind this 'I'm not the religious sort' motto.

IS THERE A RELIGIOUS SORT?

First, let me ask you, can you honestly say there is a religious sort? Don't pretend it is comprised of the effeminate, the retired and the addle-headed. I think round some of the people in our own parish church: a leading gynaecologist, a factory worker, a librarian, a horticulturalist, a garage owner, a builder, an architect, an engineer, a man who has been finding God in prison, a lawyer, an atomic scientist, a university teacher, a man on the dole, literally hundreds of students, the majority of whom are studying scientific subjects, members from Iran and India, Sri Lanka and Rhodesia, South Africa (black and white) and U.S.A., Canada and Sweden, Germany and Hong Kong, Japan and Australia, Kenya and Uganda, Sudan and Nigeria and so on. The diversity of their attitudes, their backgrounds, their educational attainments, their temperaments, their ages, their interests, their *everything*, is so vast that it would be ridiculous to class them all as the religious type. These Christians are not just one type: they are all types — extrovert and introvert, tough and weak, old and young, black and white. Their diversity has only one unifying factor, but that factor is strong as steel: Jesus Christ. Here is an example of the sort of thing I have in mind. I had a letter a few days ago from a correspondent working with *Time Magazine*. The writer tells me that he was treasurer of the Oxford Humanist Society in 1964, and was converted in 1966 largely through conviction of the Holy Spirit's presence in the life of my predecessor as Rector of St. Aldate's. He is deeply involved in the work of the church in Hong Kong at present, and is not only experiencing a deepening maturity in his own life but is also leading numerous other people to the Christ he used to reject but who is now his living Lord. Can you say that such a man was the religious sort? Can you say that the first disciples of Jesus were the religious sort? Perhaps a mystic like John was, but what of rugged, hardswearing fishermen like Andrew and Peter? What of freedom fighters like Judas Iscariot and Simon the Zealot? What of money grabbing tax collectors like Matthew? What of the drunkards and homosexuals at Corinth who became Christians? What of the thieves and magicians at Ephesus? It is ludicrous to suppose that the people who first followed Jesus belonged to the religious sort. The Jews, in fact, had a word for the religious sort; and another, far from complimentary, word for the ordinary folk, 'the people of the land'. All Jesus' first followers came from this latter group: all were the non-religious sort.

A NON-RELIGIOUS FAITH

Don't let your dislike of religion keep you away from Jesus. In a very real sense he came to destroy religion. The German martyr, Dietrich Bonhoeffer, was not playing with words when he coined the phrase 'religionless Christianity'. That is precisely what Christianity is. It is not an attempt by good-living men to please God and win a place in heaven. It is God coming in his love and generosity to seek folk who would never seek him, holding out his arms to them on a cross, and saying, 'Come to me, and let us share life together'. Not a religion, but a rescue. That is why the earliest Christians were so keen to stress that they had no temple, no altars, no priests. They had no religion in the normally accepted sense of the term: hence the Romans called them 'atheists'. Instead they had a Person, who knew them, loved them, and never left them. Nothing could separate them from his loving presence. So prayer became not a ritual but converse with a Friend. Worship was not a ceremony for Sundays but the natural outpouring of love and adoration to the Saviour by his people when they met together. They needed no churches, for where two or three were gathered together in his name, he was in their midst. They needed no priests, for Jesus had opened immediate, equal access to God's presence for every one of them. Christianity, properly understood, is the most earthy of faiths: it does not separate the secular from the sacred, but keeps the two firmly together. The Lord is as interested in what I do at eleven o'clock on Monday in my daily work as he is in what I do at eleven o'clock on Sunday in a church service.

Yes, Christianity is for non-religious people. It is not going too far to say that if you insist on being religious you will find Christianity hard, almost impossible. You will find it almost impossible to *become* a Christian, because your 'religion' will get in the way: you will feel that somehow you are better and more pleasing to God than your irreligious neighbour, and that is just what the pharisees felt — and what kept them away from Jesus. And you will find it almost impossible to *be* a Christian:

because once again your 'religion' will get in the way: you will feel that the Christian life depends on your religious observances, and not on the Lord. You will be inclined to keep a little religious corner in your life for God and not allow him to have the whole thing. You will definitely find it much harder to become and to be a Christian than the man who is not 'the religious sort'.

THE MATTER OF TRUTH

And now a few other questions for the man who is not religious. *Are you concerned about truth?* That is a vital question. Do I hear you say, 'Of course I am'? Very well, then you and the Christian are interested in just the same thing. Jesus claimed, 'I am the truth'. He claimed, in other words, to be ultimate reality in personal, human terms. If you are interested in what is ultimate and what is real, then you cannot remain disinterested in Jesus. You may examine his claims and dismiss them as untrue: what you cannot do if you maintain a deep concern for truth, is to pay him no attention, shrug your shoulders and say, 'I'm not the religious sort'.

THE MATTER OF COURAGE

Next question: *have you the courage of your convictions?* I met an atheist at a discussion group recently, an able man doing doctoral studies in physics. When we were talking personally at the end of the meeting I asked him if he had ever read one of the Gospels with an open mind, willing to respond to Christ if and when he was convinced by what he read. His reply surprised me, but on reflection I think it may be true of many others. He said, 'I dare not'. What a remarkable admission! Here was a man used to assessing material, making judgments, committing himself to theories in physics on the ground of the evidence; yet he was afraid to do the same with the New Testament material in case it should convince him and draw him to the Christ he was evading. Surely, if he had the courage of his atheistic convictions, he should have been quite willing to read the Gospels. It would give him first-hand material to make fun of with his believing friends. But no. He did not have the courage of his convictions.

The next question is very similar: *dare you take your stand with a minority?* Jesus warned potential disciples to sit down and count the cost of what following him would mean. Were they prepared to stand with 10,000 men against an opposition force of 20,000? If not, they would have to make humiliating peace terms in double quick time. It is not pleasant to admit you are wrong about the basic issues of life and death. Not easy to join the despised Christian company. Not easy to stand being mocked at work for your allegiance to Christ. Not easy to allow Christ to affect your morality. Of course it is not. Jesus never said it would be easy. He said that following him meant death as well as life. Death to the old way of living, then accepting new life, new power, new standards from the Lord. All this is very tough. Many people dress up their cowardice in quite other terms, such as indifference — 'I'm not the religious sort.' But cowardice it remains. The man of Nazareth is too demanding, too uncompromising, too loving, too upright for the soft and compromising, the lazy and those who like to go with the crowd.

THE MATTER OF FULFILMENT

Another question I would like to ask the man who is not interested in religion: *do you want to find fulfilment?* Jesus once described the Kingdom of God as finding treasure. Imagine a farmer ploughing his field, drearily, monotonously, without any special expectations. Then his ploughshare hits a box. He investigates, and finds to his amazement that the box is full of diamonds and rubies. Whose heart would not beat faster at such a discovery? That, Jesus implied, is what discovering God's kingdom is like. For the kingdom is brought to us in the person of the king; and the king is Jesus. Really, then, it is nothing to do with 'religion' and its demands and observances.

The Christian life is concerned with relationships. First comes the restoration of our relationship with God: then the restoration of our links with others, as the basic harmony brought by Christ spreads outwards. Relationships are among the most precious things in life. Yet too often they are spoiled by selfishness, racial prejudice, jealousy or pride. Jesus Christ unites people, and brings harmony where once there was discord: and that spells fulfilment at the deepest level of all.

I think of a painfully shy student who found a living faith in Christ his first weekend at the university. Within six weeks he had opened up like a flower and was relating with far greater freedom to others. I think of a couple whose marriage was on the point of breaking up, when both partners were brought to faith in Jesus. The new relationship with Christ brought them closer together than ever before, and their marriage is now strong and happy. I think of a soldier, loathed for his bigheadedness and rudeness, whose whole attitude to others changed radically when he allowed Jesus Christ to take control of him. I think of two schoolboys who could not stick each other, until both of them found Christ in the same summer holidays: thereafter relationships were on a completely new plane (I should know, for I was one of the boys). This same Jesus draws together those whom every pressure in the world is driving apart. He does it in Northern Ireland, as genuine believers (as opposed to the 'religious sort', be they Protestant or Catholic) meet across the border at nights and pray for one another, support each other's widows and tend each other's wounded. He does it in the Middle East as he brings together in one Christian fellowship the political irreconcilables, Jews and Arabs. He does it in South Africa, between white, coloured and black believers: I have seen it time and again with my own eyes. But I know no other force on earth that can do the same. Jesus is treasure indeed: for he brings fulfilment to all our relationships, once we allow him to repair our relationship to God.

THE MATTER OF DESTINY

There is one other question I would like to ask the man who is not interested in religion: *are you interested in your future?* What man is not? Our education, our aspirations, our qualification seeking, our hunger for promotion is all geared to this end — securing a better future. But what when we have got it? Is there not an emptiness at the top? Money does not satisfy permanently, nor does sex, nor does fame; nor does manipulating others. And many of the people at the top know it. The actress Raquel Welch put it well in the *Daily Express* of October 31st, 1972:

> I had acquired everything I wanted, yet I was totally miserable . . . I thought it was very peculiar that I had acquired everything I had wanted as a child — wealth, fame and accomplishment in my career. I had beautiful children, and a life style that seemed terrific, yet I was totally and miserably unhappy. I found it very frightening that one could acquire all these things and still be so miserable.

After all, what is life about? Are we bound for extinction, or is there some life beyond the grave? If you are really concerned for your future, you can scarcely avoid considering the matter of final destiny. Pascal put it at its most entertaining when he suggested that the after-life is like a wager: if you believe in God you are at no disadvantage in this life, and at considerable advantage in the next. If you do not believe, but find in the next that there *was* a next, you are most unfortunate! But to be more serious; what sense is there in shutting your eyes to the one person who is well attested as having broken the grip of death, and having come back to tell us not only that there is an after-life, but how to get there? In business or commerce it would be accounted sheer folly to go for short-term gains and neglect capital appreciation — or depreciation. Yet that is just what the man does who takes no thought for life after death. He goes for short-term goals, and takes no account of the fact that his capital, his life, is depreciating towards zero, when it could, if rightly invested, appreciate indefinitely. Christians assert, not just on the basis of documents written 2,000 years ago, but on the basis of continuing world-wide experience, that Jesus of Nazareth has broken the ultimate barrier in our universe: death. They may be right; they may not. That you must decide after investigation. But to shrug off the whole issue with 'I'm not the religious sort' is sheer folly if you think at all seriously about your future.

FAITH HAS TWO SIDES

Sometimes people say 'I'm not the religious sort' with a touch of wistfulness, rather as they say 'I wish I'd got your faith'. My answer to that is simple. You can have my faith. Faith is nothing other than trust; and trust, to be any good, must have two sides to it. First, there needs to be good evidence of trustworthiness; then there needs to be genuine commitment. It is as simple as that. You have faith in Rolls Royce engines when you fly in a jet, do you not? That means that in your opinion Rolls Royce engines are reliable; it also means that you are prepared to entrust yourself to their trustworthiness. So it is with Christianity. You need first to be convinced that there is a God, that he cares about mankind, that he has revealed himself in Jesus Christ, and that it is possible for you to get in touch with him. Then you need to entrust yourself to his trust-worthiness.

In the pages that follow we shall be considering the various topics in a progression which will, I hope, help you both to appreciate the trustworthiness of God and also encourage you to entrust yourself to it. Then you will have my faith. Then you will be able to say 'I'm not the religious sort, but I think I have discovered the key to the universe.'

3

'You can't believe in God these days'

GOD IS OUT OF FASHION

Despite the opinion polls, which show that the majority of people in Western countries (not to mention the overwhelming majority in the East) do believe in God, it is amazing how often you hear the question of the Almighty dismissed in a single sentence, 'Oh, you can't believe in God these days.'

Very understandable in a way. We live in a very busy age, and many of us have neither the time nor the inclination to enquire into abstruse subjects which do not directly concern us. But what if there is a God who made us, loves us and will judge us? Well, if that is the case, as Dr. Jowett, famous head of an Oxford college once put it, 'It is not what I think of God, but what God thinks of me that matters.'

Again, the idea of God has been so abused in the past that we tend to shy away from it. God has been portrayed as the man in the sky with the big stick. We have been told to be good and to do the right thing because God would judge us if we offended. God's will has been found a very useful tool for keeping people in their places:

> The rich man in his castle,
> The poor man at his gate;
> God made them high and lowly,
> And ordered their estate.

A whole system of social and racial oppression has been founded on that view of God (a verse from the hymn 'All things bright and beautiful', now generally omitted). Indeed, God's will is something which certain people in certain ages have claimed to be so sure about that they have engaged in religious wars, like the Crusades, or religious persecutions, like the Inquisition, to press their point. God has, furthermore, been used as a sort of plug to fill gaps in scientific knowledge: even Newton postulated God to keep the universe and its laws going. But as scientific knowledge has grown, the gaps have shrunk and God with them.

For all these reasons God is out of fashion. As *Time Magazine* headlined on its cover in April 1966, *God is Dead!* But it is difficult to be sure about these things. Perhaps there is as much fashion as there is reason about it all, for in December 1969 the headlines of *Time Magazine* were asking, *Is God Coming to Life Again?* After all, you get no justification for religious wars or inquisitions in the Bible. You do not find this handbook of Christianity maintaining that you should do good in case God should punish you for your failures. God is nowhere used in the Bible to plug the gaps in human knowledge: rather, he is portrayed as the source and sustainer and goal of the whole universe, including man and his knowledge. Perhaps we ought to look a little more closely at this claim that you can't believe these days. What is so special about these days that makes it harder for us to believe in God than it was for our fathers?

THE PROBLEM OF SCIENCE

First, there's the astonishing success of science. In the past fifty years the whole face of the world has changed. When my father was a boy there were no cars, no aeroplanes, and most people never moved more than a few miles from their own village. The change to space travel, nuclear technology, and the global village has all happened in his lifetime. No wonder men are confused. Science would seem to have won the day. No wonder many people pin all their hopes on it, and discard the idea of God. Sir Richard Gregory wrote his own epitaph:

> My grandfather preached the gospel of Christ.
> My father preached the gospel of socialism.
> I preach the gospel of science.

In point of fact, there is no battle between an informed belief in God and the assured results of science. The fathers of modern science, men like Kepler, Galileo, Copernicus and Bacon were earnest believers in God. They saw God's revelation in Scripture and in the natural world as complementary. Kepler, for instance, asserted. 'The tongue of God and the finger of God cannot clash.' The Cavendish Laboratory in Cambridge has inscribed above its entrance: 'The works of the Lord are great, sought out by all who have pleasure therein.' And, contrary to the belief of many, there is a high proportion of believing Christians among the leading scientists of the world.

But doesn't evolution rule out the possibility of a Creator? Far from it. The theory of evolution sets out to explain how varied forms of life have developed from more simple forms over millions of years. Belief in a Creator sets out to explain the great Mind behind all matter. There is no contradiction between the two. Interestingly enough, the Bible account of God's creation tells us something of the One who created, and something of why he did it. But it does not set out to tell us how. The world may have originated in a big bang or in a steady state; our first parents may have been developed from a collateral stock with monkeys or they may not. This is not a matter on which the Bible has anything to say. What it does say is that behind the creature lies the Creator, and that we are not only 'of the dust of the ground', and part of the physical universe, but are also in some sense infused with 'the breath of life' and made in the Creator's image. No discoveries in the realm of how life developed can repudiate that claim. If man discovers how to create life in a laboratory that would not put God out of business. It would simply show that when brilliant minds take matter (with real living matter to copy, incidentally) and arrange it in a very special way, a living particle may come into existence. In other words, matter arranged by intelligent minds can produce life. Exactly what Christians have always claimed for God. If we discover the secret of life, we shall merely be thinking the Creator's thoughts after him.

There is nothing in the scientific method that can either demonstrate God's existence or disprove it. But, for what it is worth, the basic presupposition of the scientific method strongly supports the existence of a Mind behind matter. It is axiomatic for all scientific enquiry that there is order and purpose in the physical world. Why should this be if the world sprang from chance and chaos? There are very few pure materialists around these days, for it is abundantly obvious that analysis of physical laws and chemical constituents cannot explain human behaviour, reason, emotion, wonder, speech, morals and worship. 'There are more things in heaven and earth than are dreamed of by your philosophy': these words of Shakespeare are applicable to the man who tries to make scientific materialism the only arbiter of truth. There is nothing in scientific procedure, still less in the theory of evolution, that need embarrass any believer in God the Creator.

THE PROBLEM OF SUFFERING

Second, there's the ghastly problem of suffering. Not that it is greater than ever before, but it seems greater. It is brought into the living room every night on T.V. How can there be a God if he allows all this pain and anguish in his world?

I do not want to minimise this problem for one moment. It is by far the strongest argument against the existence of God. But suppose for a minute that the problem of pain drives you to reject God's existence and to imagine that either some monster rules our destinies or that the stars are in charge of our fortunes, how does that help? You may have got rid of the problem of evil and pain (though you still have to live with them) but you have replaced them with a much bigger problem; how you get kindness and humanity, love and unselfishness, gentleness and goodness in a world that is governed by a horrid monster or uncaring stars. No, that way does not help.

As a matter of fact the Christian has a greater insight into the insoluble problem of suffering (and it remains insoluble, whatever philosophy of life you take up) than anyone else. For the Scriptures teach us that God is no stranger to pain. He did not start the world off and leave it callously to its own devices. He does not willingly afflict us, and take delight in torturing us. The very reverse. He cares so much about the agony and pain of this struggling world of his that he has got involved in it personally. He came as a man among men. He lived in squalor and suffering; he knew thirst and hunger, flogging and heart-break, fear and despair. He ended his life in one of the most excruciating ways known to man. Let nobody tell me that God doesn't care! Let nobody claim that the boss doesn't know what life is like on the shop floor!

Take a long hard look at the cross. Through that cross God is saying to you that he does care about pain. He cares passionately and selflessly. He cares so much that he came to share it.

He is for ever the Suffering God. The cross tells me that God loves me even in the midst of pain and suffering; when everything looked at its blackest Jesus was still the supreme object of his Heavenly Father's love. More, through that cross I can vaguely discern another truth: that God uses pain. He turns evil into good. For it was evil, real evil, that crucified Jesus. And yet by the way he took it he overcame evil; he turned hatred to love in some at least of his persecutors. He gave an example of innocent, uncomplaining suffering which has inspired men ever since, and enabled men like Bishop Wilson to win the hearts of some of the men who tortured him in a Japanese prison camp in the Second World War by means of his courage and spirit. And what makes such overcoming of pain possible? Not merely the cross of Jesus as an example to follow. One needs more than an example in the midst of agony. There was something else about the cross which has rubbed off on Christians ever since. It is the sense of victory. On the first Good Friday Jesus died with a cry of triumph on his lips: triumph over pain and hatred, suffering and death. And that was not the end. He rose from the chill grip of the tomb on the third day. From that moment onwards he enjoys the power of an endless life. Christians are people who have put their trust in him, come to know him, and begun to taste the power of his risen and endless life. How is it that the early Christians could look cheerfully at death in the arena from wild beasts and gladiators or being roasted on a grid? Simply because they were convinced that evil and pain had suffered a crucial defeat through what God did on that cross of Calvary and the resulting resurrection. Even death was a defeated foe. So they came to look on suffering not as an unmitigated evil, but as an evil which had been conquered by their suffering and triumphant God; an evil which he could even use to discipline them, to refine them, and to equip them for further usefulness and deeper Christlikeness. And the suffering but victorious God, the sinless but sinbearing God, has given on the cross of Christ a trailer of his future film. They could safely leave him to give fuller light on it all in the life to come, knowing that it would be a further explanation of the mystery of the cross, where, in the very midst of history, God showed that he cared about pain, shared it, and overcame it. To be sure, the Christian need not be worried that suffering in the world makes belief in God impossible these days. It is only belief in a suffering God that stops us from either becoming totally callous or going out of our minds at all the suffering which afflicts our world.

THE PROBLEM OF MEANINGLESSNESS

Third, there's the problem of meaninglessness. Never before in the history of mankind has there been such a widespread belief that in the end nothing matters; we came from nothing and we go to nothing. No values are implanted in us because there is no God to implant them; no part of the human frame survives death, because there is no eternity. Meaning has disappeared from life. More money, more leisure, yes: but don't talk to us about meaning in life, because there isn't any. A leading modern painter, Francis Bacon writes:

> Man now realises that he is an accident, that he is a completely futile being, that he has to play out the game without reason. Earlier artists were still conditioned by certain types of religious possibilities, which man now, you could say, has had cancelled out for him. Man can now only attempt to beguile himself for a time by prolonging his life — by buying a kind of immortality through the doctors ... The artist must really deepen the game to be any good at all, so that he can make life a bit more exciting.

What in fact the artist has done is to bring home this meaninglessness to every level of society. It comes through the films and the pop music. It is everywhere. Take David Crosby's song *If only I could remember my name*:

> I thought I met a man who knew a man who knew what was
> going on

I was mistaken — only another stranger that I knew.
I thought I'd found a light to guide me through the night and
    all its darkness
I was mistaken — only reflections of a shadow that I saw.
I thought I'd seen someone who seemed at last to know the
    truth
I was mistaken — only a child laughing in the sun.

Running to sex seems to be the way out of meaninglessness: but
no. This extract from the sex novel *Naked as the Wind from
the Sea* is typical:

> Everyone is confused after our last catastrophe. We are
> like ants whose stack has been taken away: we run around in
> all directions with the straw and want to build a new one. But
> they've taken away our meaning. All we can do is to struggle
> with our straw just the same . . .

Now if you are eaten up with this philosophy of meaninglessness, of course you won't find any sense in God talk. But
it is a chicken and egg situation. The philosophy of meaninglessness is an attempt by modern existentialists to draw the
full consequences from atheism. Deny God, and then see if you
can make sense of everything else. And the fact is that you
can't.

But try it the other way around. What if there is a God?
Then the world is not a mere fluke; it is the result of his creation. Man is not rubbish, but God's deputy on this earth. History is not bunk, but God's story struggling for expression
through all the follies of mankind. Life is not meant to be
understood simply in terms of the three score years and ten, but
as a training ground for being with God for ever. No longer
need we be torn between the very obvious order and purpose in
nature and the purposelessness, the meaningless lostness which
modern man finds in his heart. If modern man will return to the
Creator of order and purpose in nature, he will begin to find
order coming through in his own life, and a sense of purpose in
co-operating with the Creator in the management of his world.

THE PROBLEM OF PROOF

The fourth problem is the matter of proof. 'You can't prove God,' they say. Perfectly true. You can't. But you can't prove that your mother loves you, either. In fact, there are precious few things that you can prove, and they are by no means the most interesting things in life. To prove a thing really means to show that it could not be otherwise, a very final form of certainty. You cannot prove that the sun will rise tomorrow. You cannot prove that you are alive. You cannot prove the link between cause and effect which runs through every action we do. You cannot prove that you are the same man you were ten years ago. The philosopher, David Hume, attempted to prove the link between cause and effect and between himself as he then was and himself ten years previously, and he failed. Failed utterly. Proof is only applicable to very rarefied areas of philosophy and mathematics and even here there is debate. For the most part we are driven to acting on good evidence, without the luxury of proof. There is good evidence of the link between cause and effect. There is good evidence that the sun will rise tomorrow. There is good reason to believe that I am the same man as I was ten years ago. There is good reason to suppose that my mother really loves me and is not just fattening me up for the moment when she will pop arsenic into my tea. And there is good reason to believe in God. Very good reason. Not conclusive proof, but very good reason just the same. Let me outline to you why I believe it is much harder to reject the existence of a supreme being than to accept it.

1. THE FACT OF THE WORLD

Look at the fact of the world. So far as we know at present, this planet is the only part of the universe where there is life. What accounts for this world of ours? Whether we go for the 'Big Bang' theory or the 'Steady State' theory, we are driven to ask *why* it should be so? The world must have come from somewhere. It will not do to reply 'It is just one of those things.' It will not do to assign the whole thing to chance. If the world is due to chance, how is it that cause and effect are built into that world at every turn? It isn't very rational to suppose that chance gives birth to cause and effect! And it isn't very rational to argue that the world which is based on cause and effect is itself uncaused. Huxley once said, 'The link between cause and effect is the chief article in the scientist's creed.' If you think hard enough, science itself drives you back to believe in a Creator.

2. THE FACT OF DESIGN

Look at the fact of design. At every level the world of nature shows evidence of design. Think of the focusing equipment of an eye, of the radar of a bat, of the built-in gyroscope of a swallow, of the camouflage of a nesting pheasant. Or think of the perfect harmony of the laws of physics. Reflect on the marvel of conception and birth. At every point there is evidence of a great Designer. Even John Stuart Mill, a strong opponent of Christianity, came to the conclusion at the end of his life that 'the argument from design is irresistible. Nature does testify to its creator.' Einstein, too, spoke of his 'humble admiration for the illimitably superior Spirit who reveals himself in the slight details which we can perceive with our frail mind.' After Einstein had propounded his theory of relativity, and after its general acceptance following the Michelson–Morley experiment, the experiment was repeated and gave different results. But nobody doubted the relativity theory! Everyone assumed (rightly as it turned out) that the results must be due to experimental error, because the theory was too good, *too rational*, to be false. In other words, the physicists themselves were operating on the assumption of design in the universe, however much they might have claimed to be following merely experimental results.

Very well then, if there is design in the world, where did it come from? Not from us: we don't lay down the laws of nature or design the development of the foetus in the womb. It looks very much as though a Designer is at work.

Long ago Paley developed the argument by means of a watch. It runs something like this. 'See this watch? Well, in the old days people used to believe that a watchmaker had made it. The cogs, the pinions, the glass and numbers all bore the marks of intelligent design. But now we have grown out of that sort of thing. We know that a watch has gradually evolved. There is no design about it. Natural selection has slowly eliminated all elements that are irrelevant to watches. The metal has coalesced, the glass has grown over, the cogs have gradually developed, and last of all the strap grew.' Put like this it is not difficult to see how ridiculous the argument is; the man who advanced it would be ignored, if not hastily hustled into a mental hospital! Yet precisely the same argument is advanced about the world itself by sane men who think they are being both reasonable and avant-garde. To attribute marks of design to blind evolution makes no more sense in the case of the world than it does in the case of the watch. Paley's argument has been attacked on the ground that God is not a watchmaker. True, but Paley never said he was. God is far more than a watchmaker, if he is God at all. But he is assuredly not less! The argument from design is extremely persuasive, and to say with Jean-Paul Sartre, 'This world is not the product of Intelligence. It meets our gaze as would a crumpled piece of paper . . . What is man but a little puddle of water whose freedom is death?' is to shut your eyes to one of the clearest indications that there is a Creator God who has not left himself without witness. 'The heavens declare the glory of God and the firmament shows his handiwork' remains true: so does the Bible's assertion 'The fool has said in his heart, "There is no God."' (Psalm 19: 1, and 14: 1).

3. THE FACT OF PERSONALITY

Look at the fact of personality. It is one of the most remarkable phenomena in the world. The difference between a person and a thing, between a live person and a dead one, is fundamental. When Sartre, in the quotation given above, denied that the world was created by Intelligence, he was not only insulting his Maker but his own power of reasoning. He was saying, in effect, that there was no reason to believe what he was saying! The fact is that we are not mere robots; there is more to us than that — human personality. Some thinkers are so reluctant to believe this that they have advanced the improbable creed of materialism, seeking to reduce everything in life to what can be measured scientifically. In other words, other people are mere blobs of protoplasm: so am I. I have no future, no real existence. I think I am a conscious, rational being who can mix with others like me. But no. Science knows nothing of rationality and consciousness, of personality and sociability. It deals only with molecules and magnestism, elements and electricity, things which can be counted and measured. I have no place in such language, and if that is the ultimate language of reality, then I cannot describe myself, and am driven to the conclusion that I do not exist. Not very plausible. But the alternative is disturbing. It suggests that my personality cannot be explained simply in terms of its physical components. I am more than matter. Very well, but how come, if there is no God? Does a river run higher than its source? Of course not. Then how do we get human personality out of the inorganic matter which is the brute stuff of which our universe is entirely composed, in the atheist view? Can rationality and life spring from chance and non-being? No, the fact of human personality is another impressive pointer to the God who created a man in his own image. This is not to say that God is restricted to a personality like ours: but it is to say that the ultimate source of our being is not less than personal.

4. THE FACT OF VALUES

Look at the fact of values. We all have them, but they are very hard to understand if there is no God. After all, you don't expect to find values knocking around in molecules! Matter does not give rise to morals. So modern Godless man is confused about where his values fit in. That comes across clearly in

The Who's record *The Seeker*, 'I've got values, but I don't know how or why'. We value life — but why should we if life really springs from chance? We value truth — but why should we if there is no ultimate reality? We value goodness — but what is that doing in a world derived from plankton? We revel in beauty — but there is nothing in it, since it too springs from the chaos in which our world originated. We value communication — but the universe is silent. Yes, we have our values, and they do not accord very well with the atheist's picture of the world, sprung merely from chance, matter, and millions of years to allow for extensive development. I do not find much basis for value judgments there.

But what if there is a Creator God? Then life is valuable because it is his greatest gift, hence the infinite value of every individual. Truth matters because it is one aspect of God, the ultimate reality. Beauty and goodness are likewise two of the 'faces' of God, and every good action or beautiful sight is an inkling of the good and beautiful source from which they come. Best of all, we do not inhabit a silent planet: God has spoken and revealed himself, to some extent at least, in the world, in its design, in values and in man. When we communicate it is not vain jabbering but a God-given ability, entrusted to us by the great Communicator himself. Those are two basic attitudes to values. I know which makes more sense to me. John Lucas, the Oxford philosopher, develops this argument clearly and simply:

> I want to do well. But it is impossible to do well unless there are values independent of me by which my performance can be assessed. I cannot want to do only what I want to do, or I am denying my nature as a rational agent. I must want to do what is worth doing, and what is worth doing is so not because I want it, but because independently of my desires, and whether I wish it or no.

The existence of values is a pointer to God which it is hard, indeed, to evade.

5. THE FACT OF CONSCIENCE

Look at the fact of conscience. That's a pointer to God if ever there was one. Your conscience doesn't argue. It acts like a law-giver inside you, acquitting you or condemning you. It doesn't say, 'Do this because you will gain by it' or 'Do it because you will escape trouble that way.' It just says, 'Do it.' It is a most remarkable pointer to the God who put it there. Oh, of course it is not the voice of God straight and simple. It has been warped by all sorts of things, your environment, your rationalisations, your disobedience. But equally certainly conscience can't just be explained away as the pressure of society. It was not from any pressure by society that Newton and Wilberforce con-scientiously fought for the liberation of slaves, or Martin Luther King championed the cause of the blacks. Their action was carried out in the teeth of opposition by society, and so it has always been with every moral advance.

Despite the diversity of human cultures the world over, there is actually remarkable agreement on the essential values to which conscience points: the general condemnation of murder and theft, of adultery and lust, of hijacking and hate. There is universal agreement that peace is right and war is wrong; that love is right and hate is wrong — however little men manage to carry it out in practice. And it is conscience that points us to this difference between right and wrong, and the claim that right has upon us. C. S. Lewis summed it up like this:

> If no set of moral ideas were better than another, there would be no sense in preferring civilised morality to Nazi morality. The moment you say one lot of morals is better than another, you are in fact measuring them by an ultimate standard.

Even Bertrand Russell, who during the earlier part of his life fought tooth and nail against the idea of an ultimate distinction between right and wrong, said, towards the end of his life, 'To love is right, to hate is wrong.' But how does he get such moral absolutes in what he claimed is a Godless world? It doesn't add up. You do not locate principles of conscience in a chance collection of atoms, which is all the world consists of if you remove the possibility of a Creator. No; morality, conscience, the difference between right and wrong are important indicators of a God who is interested in what is right and good and true. He is no blind force, no abstruse designer, but a personal God, so concerned with what is right that he has built a moral indicator into each one of his creatures.

6. THE FACT OF RELIGION

Look at the fact of religion. Man is a religious animal. In the sixth century B.C. philosophers in Greece poured scorn on religion, and invited men to grow up. Religion continued. And so it has done everywhere in the world ever since. The Russians sought to abolish religion after the Revolution in 1917. They failed. They tried again with violent persecution under Stalin. They failed. It is the same in China. Man is incurably religious. He is going to worship either God or a pseudo-god, but worship something he will, even if it is something very physical like his material prosperity or something very abstract like the idea of progress.

There is one fact about man that has distinguished him from his first appearance on earth. It marks him as different from all other creatures. That is, he's a worshipping animal. Wherever he has existed there are the remains, in some form or other, of his worship. That's not a pious conclusion: it's an observed fact. And all through history and prehistory when he's deprived himself of that he's gone to pieces. Many people nowadays are going to pieces, or they find the first convenient prop to tie their instincts on to. It's behind the extraordinary adulation of royalty. It's behind the mobbing of T.V. stars. If you don't give an expression to an instinct you've got to sublimate it or go out of your mind.

Such is the conclusion not of a philosopher or priest, but of a novelist, Winston Graham in *The Sleeping Partner*. He's right, isn't he?

These are some of the facts that, taken together, not only make belief in God reasonable, but make it very hard indeed rationally to deny his existence. They point to a God who is skilful, skilful enough to design the courses of the stars and the development of a foetus. They point to a God who is the source of human personality, and therefore not less than personal however much he may transcend all that we mean by that word. He is the ultimate source of our values: life and language, truth, beauty and goodness find their ultimate home in him. He is so concerned about right and wrong that he has furnished each of his creatures with a conscience. And he wants us to know him and to enjoy him, to worship and to live in his company — hence the universal religious instinct of men through history and throughout the world.

But he still remains the Unknown God. How are we to discover any more about him? Perhaps all religions lead to God. Let us examine that possibility in our next chapter.

4

'All religions lead to God'

AN ATTRACTIVE THEORY

UNTIL A FEW years ago comparative religion was a study for the handful of experts who busied themselves in such an odd subject. Now it is replacing the study of theology in universities all over the Western world and has a firm niche in religious instruction in schools. The reason, of course, is that we have at last woken up to the fact that the world is a global village, and the influx of Asians, Indians, Arabs and Pakistanis into Britain has meant that the problem of other religions has landed on our own doorstep. What are we to make of these other faiths? Presumably they are all much of a muchness. Presumably they are all pathways to God, and you might as well take your pick.

Such a view has immense attractions. It avoids the black and white choice and sees everything as a shade of grey. It is essentially tolerant, and tolerance is a very fashionable virtue. It is modest, and does not make strong pretensions for your own particular religion. It seems admirable common sense. We take the views of everybody, and try to build up an Identikit picture of God. And some extremely significant people and organisations back it up. For example the saintly Indian leader Mahatma Gandhi said, 'The soul of religions is one, but it is encased in a multitude of forms . . . Truth is the exclusive property of no single scripture . . . I cannot ascribe exclusive divinity to Jesus. He is as divine as Krishna or Rama or Mohammed or Zoroaster.' The Hindu mystic Ramakrishna used to speak of himself as the same soul that has been born before as Rama, as Krishna, as Jesus or as Buddha. The Roman Emperor Severus hedged his bets by having in his private chapel not only the statues of the deified emperors, but those of the miracle-worker Apollonius of Tyana, of Christ, of Abraham and of Orpheus! A very contemporary attitude, as this song of Quintessence makes plain:

> Jesus, Buddha, Moses, Gauranga,
> Draw me deep in the sea of your love
> Jesus, Buddha, Moses, Gauranga,
> Oh maya, oh maya, oh maya.

A very common view then — but it won't do, for two compelling reasons.

IT'S ILLOGICAL

It is a lovely sentimental idea to suppose that all religions are basically one, and that they all represent variations on a common theme. But unfortunately it flies in the face of all the evidence. How can all religions lead to God when they are so different? The God of Hinduism is plural and impersonal. The God of Islam is singular and personal. The God of Christianity is the Creator of the world. The divine in Buddhism is not personal and is not creative. You could scarcely have a greater contrast than that. Christianity teaches that God both forgives a man and gives him supernatural aid. In Buddhism there is no forgiveness, and no supernatural aid. The goal of all existence in Buddhism is *nirvana*, extinction — attained by the Buddha after no less than 547 births. The goal of all existence in Christianity is to know God and enjoy him for ever. The use of images figures prominently in Hinduism: Judaism prohibits making any image of God. Islam allows a man four wives; Christianity one. Perhaps the greatest difference of all lies between the Bible, which asserts that nobody can save himself and make himself pleasing to God, try as he will; and almost all the other faiths which assert that by keeping their teachings a man will be saved or reborn or made whole or achieve fulfilment. Nothing spells out this contrast more powerfully than the Buddhist story which starts off so like the parable of the Prodigal Son. The boy comes home and is met by the father, and then has to work off the penalty for his past misdeeds by years of servitude to his father. The principle of *karma* (cause and effect, paying off your guilt) is poles apart from grace (free forgiveness when you don't deserve it a bit).

I do not at this point want to evaluate different religious faiths. I just want to show how utterly illogical it is to say that they are all pointing in the same direction. It is as foolish as to say that all roads from Nottingham lead to London. They do nothing of the sort, and it is not helpful in the least to pretend that they do. They lead to radically different goals. Extinction or heaven; pardon or paying it off; a personal God or an impersonal monad; salvation by grace or by works. The contrasts are irreconcilable.

The trouble is that today's tolerance has reached the point where it is no longer a virtue but a vice. It is a cruel casualness to truth. It is no kindness to anyone if we tell everyone that their views are as true as anyone else's. We are simply displaying our cynicism, as if we said to a blind man sitting on the edge of a precipice, 'It doesn't matter which way you move. All paths lead to the same goal.'

Lesslie Newbigin, Christian bishop in Madras, has been forced to examine very carefully the difference between Christianity and other faiths. How could he help it, living in the midst of a Hindu culture? He puts it like this in his remarkable book, *The Finality of Christ*. The great divide among religions, he maintains, is their attitude to history. Most religions are like a wheel. 'The cycle of birth, growth, decay and death through which plants, animals, human beings and institutions all pass suggests a rotating wheel — ever in movement yet ever returning upon itself.' The wheel offers one way of escape from the meaningless, repetitive movement it generates. That is to take a spoke — it cannot matter which one — and travel along it to the hub, where all is at rest, and where you can observe the ceaseless movement without being involved in it. This is the way of most religions: 'dispute among the different "ways" is pointless; all that matters is that those who follow them should find their way to that timeless, motionless centre where all is peace, and where one can understand all the endless movement which makes up human history — understand that it goes nowhere and means nothing.'

The other great symbol is not a wheel but a road. This is the view of Judaism and Christianity. Newbigin expresses it thus:

> History is a journey, a pilgrimage. We do not yet see the goal, but we believe in it and seek it. The movement in which we are involved is not meaningless movement; it is movement towards a goal. The goal ... is not a timeless reality hidden behind the multiplicity and change which we experience. It is yet to be achieved; it lies at the end of the road.

That is the uniqueness of the Christian claim. God has intervened in history. The history of the Jewish people, the birth of

Jesus, the cross and the resurrection are milestones along that road which ends in heaven.

Not only, then, is it illogical to suppose that all religions lead to God: it is impossible.

IT'S IMPOSSIBLE

There are two reasons why it is impossible for us to find God through whatever religion you care to name. The first is because of the nature of God. If there is a God, then he is the source of both man and his environment. He is the Lord over all human life.

> Have you not known? Have you not heard? Has it not been told you from the beginning? It is he who sits above the circle of the earth, and its inhabitants are like grasshoppers ... Whom did he consult for his enlightenment, and who taught him the path of knowledge and showed him the way of understanding? Behold, the nations are like a drop from a bucket, and are accounted as dust on the scales; behold he takes up the isles like fine dust (Isaiah 40: 21ff).

That is the God we are talking about. How can we possibly climb up to him? How can the cup understand the potter who made it? It cannot be done. Man cannot find out God however hard he searches. Religion, all religion, is bound to fail.

As we have seen, we can have a go at it. But how far does it get us? The facts we considered in the last chapter get us a little way along the line, but only a very little way, and they amount to not much more than conjecture. The fact of the world indicates an outside cause. Design in the world suggests this cause's intelligence. The fact of human life suggests that this cause is not only intelligent but personal. Conscience indicates his concern about right conduct, and values like truth, beauty and goodness may have their origin in him. The fact that no nation in the world has lived without belief in God suggests that God wants man's worship.

But so what? He remains the unknown God. You can get so far by inference, but no further. After that you need to hear from him, or meet him — or both. The creature cannot possibly discover the Creator, unless he chooses to disclose himself. That is one reason why all religions are bound to disappoint. And as a matter of fact that is precisely what they all do.

Christopher Mayhew published a book some years ago, entitled *Men in Search of God*. In it, representatives of various world religions gave their account of their religious experience, and their search for God. Not surprisingly, none of them claimed to have found him. Gordon Bailey puts it epigrammatically in his little poem *If*.

> If
> all religions
> lead to God
> how come
> most of them,
> having been given
> a thousand years at least,
> haven't yet
> arrived?

If by 'religion' we mean man's search for the divine, it is bound to fail. What we need is not to compare the chinks of light that each of us may have grasped, but for the day to dawn. We need not a religion but a revelation. And that is precisely what Christianity claims to be. A revelation from God. Unlike other holy books, the Bible does not bring us the story of men in search of God; it tells us about the God who comes in search of men.

No THROUGH ROAD

There is a second reason why religion will never win through to God. Not simply because of the nature of God, but because of the nature of man. The Bible gives a pretty unflattering picture of man, but one that is uncomfortably near the mark. It tells us several unpleasing truths.

For instance, it informs us that we are not the earnest lovers of God that we would like to suppose: on the contrary, we are 'enemies in our minds by wicked deeds'. We do not have that heart of gold which we like to think we have: on the contrary 'the heart of man is deceitful above all things and desperately sick'. It tells us that we are not impartial in our search for the truth: on the contrary, 'men suppress the truth in unrighteous living'. We do not follow every gleam of light that comes our way: on the contrary, 'men love darkness rather than light because their deeds are evil' (Colossians 1: 21, Jeremiah 17: 9, Romans 1: 18, John 3: 19).

There seems to be a basic twist in human nature which makes us incapable of welcoming the best when we see it. More often than not we want to get rid of it, because it shows us up. One of the more pathetic illusions of humanism is that men are all good folk at heart, and given decent environment, decent working conditions, plenty of money and secure employment they will all be good citizens, and the heart of gold will shine out. What rubbish! If we are all good folk at heart why does the crime rate go up every year along with our prosperity? (In London it has increased twenty fold in the last fifty years, and in a recent survey ninety per cent of London youngsters under sixteen admitted they had at some time or other engaged in theft). If we were all good folk at heart, how we would flock to the best person there has ever been, Jesus Christ. But anyone who has had any experience in evangelism, in bringing others to share in the joy of the Christian life, knows what a battle generally ensues before the person in question finally gives in to Christ. I have seen 'good' men sweating with the intensity of their struggle to keep clear of the Light of the world. Francis Thompson knew what he was talking about in that poem of his, *The Hound of Heaven,* which begins:

> I fled him down the nights and down the days
> I fled him down the arches of the years

I fled him down the labyrinthine ways
Of my own mind, and in the mist of tears
I hid from him, and under running laughter.

The very fact that we hide from him shows that we are self-centred creatures at heart, just as the Bible says we are. And we have another closely allied problem. There is something wrong with our will. We don't seem to be able to live up even to our own occasional efforts after high standards. How long do your New Year resolutions last, for instance? How long does that peace and goodwill of the Christmas period continue in your office? Or how many times have you given up smoking? Jesus put his finger on the trouble when he said, 'Whoever does wrong becomes a slave of wrong.'

No wonder Paul comes to the conclusion that the Old Testament had reached before him, as he draws to the end of his shattering indictment of contemporary pagan and religious society. 'There is none righteous, no, not one. There is none that understands and seeks after God' (Romans 3: 10, 11). The myth is exploded. We are not honest seekers after God. Most of us, most of the time, are only too thankful to keep out of his way. All men are disqualified, whether they come from the so-called Christian West, the Communist bloc or the mystic East. None have arrived at God, both because he is too great for any of his creatures to pierce his incognito; and because his creatures are too twisted, too self-centred to want to. The greatness of God and the sinfulness of man are two massive barriers to our supposing that all religions lead to God. They do nothing of the sort. No religions lead to him.

ONLY ONE HOPE

There is only one hope, and that is the possibility of revelation. We cannot reach God, but there is no reason why he should not reach us. That is a consideration which escaped the celebrated Herbert Spencer, a leading agnostic. He maintained, sensibly enough, that no man has ever been known to penetrate with his finite mind the veil which hides the mind of the Infinite. He concluded that the Infinite could not be known by the finite, and that agnosticism was therefore secure. Not at all. There is no reason why the Infinite should not make himself known to the finite, and the Bible gives the account of the only faith which claims that he has done precisely that.

A REVELATION

Suppose for a moment you were God. The people you had made have turned their backs on you. They do not want to share their lives with you. They want to go their own way. What are you to do? You might start with a likely individual, and work on him and his descendents. God did that: the likely individual was called Abraham. He trusted God, obeyed him, and became the father of the Jewish nation. But that nation strayed away from the path Abraham had trodden. What was to be done? Perhaps a time of hardship in a foreign and oppressive country might make them come to their senses? That is what Israel's time in Egypt was all about, and later on the medicine had to be repeated in the Babylonian exile. You might raise up prophets to call the people back to yourself. God did just that, too. 'Listen to the words of my servants the prophets,' says the Lord, 'whom I sent unto you, rising up early and sending them ... but you have not listened.' Finally, if you cared enough, you might come in person, for a sort of summit visit, after your staff had sufficiently prepared the way. That, too, God did at the first Christmas. The way was as prepared as it could be. The Jewish nation after two thousand years of history was passionately persuaded that there was one God, and no runners up. The Roman Empire had secured peace throughout the known world. The Greek language was universal, and its culture pervasive. The stage was set for the maximum impact of God's personal visit. And so the one called Jesus ('God the rescuer'), or Emmanuel ('God is with us'), was born. The God who had over many centuries and in many different ways spoken through his prophets to the people, had at last spoken a clear, final and decisive message, not through a prophet but in the person of his Son. At long last men could see that God is, God speaks, God cares. No longer is he the unknown God. 'No man has seen God at any time, but the only begotten one, himself God, has made him known' was how one eyewitness summed the matter up (John 1: 18). Jesus shows us in terms of a human life what God is like. That was the first purpose of his coming to our world, to bring us the revelation of God without which we would still be fumbling vainly in the dark.

A RESCUE

His coming had a second purpose, as well, closely linked with the first. For when mankind saw that perfect life of uprightness and love, the highest and the best imaginable, they nailed him to a cross. He was too uncomfortable. His was too blazing a light. The natural instinct of mankind who likes living in the dark was, and is, to extinguish that embarrassing light. They did not succeed, of course. 'The light goes on shining in the darkness, and the darkness did not quench it,' but they had a jolly good try. Do you see what happened? The coming of Jesus did not merely show us what God is like. It also showed up what man is like. 'Men loved darkness rather than light because their deeds were evil,' wrote St. John; and if you want commentary on that verse ask yourself what would happen to the circulation of the Sunday papers if they started recording acts of virtue rather than deeds of vice! There you have clear evidence that men love darkness rather than light. So we human beings need something more basic even than a revelation from God. We need a rescue by God.

Not only our understanding but our will is at fault. Jesus came to rectify both. He showed us what God was like by his incomparable life. He put us right with God by his sacrificial death. That is why the cross is the symbol of Christianity. It is the most important achievement of the whole of his life, indeed in the whole of history. There Jesus, the God-man, took responsibility for all the evil of mankind. 'He suffered for sins,

the just for the unjust, so as to bring us to God,' said one
eyewitness (1 Peter 3: 18). 'Herein is love, not that we loved
God, but that he loved us, and sent his Son to be the remedy for
the defilement of our sins,' writes another (1 John 4: 10).
Another New Testament writer cries out in exultation, 'There
is now no condemnation for the man who is united to Christ'
(Romans 8: 1) because 'God sending his own Son in the like-
ness of human flesh, and as a sin offering, condemned sin in the
flesh [i.e. of Christ].' Wherever you look in the New Testament
you find the same truth, however variously it is expressed. In
the pictorial language of the Book of Revelation you find it put
like this: 'I saw a great multitude, whom no man could number,
of all nations and kindreds and peoples and tongues stand
before the throne and before the Lamb, clothed with white
robes, and palms in their hands, saying with a loud voice "Salvation belongs to our God who sits on the throne and to the
Lamb" ' (Revelation 7: 9, 10).

NOTHING LIKE IT

The symbolism is plain. These people from every background
in the world are praising God in heaven, and thanking him for
his rescue operation that covers the scruffy clothes of their fancied goodness with the perfect white robe of Christ's righteousness. As the writer goes on to say a few verses later, 'These are
they who have washed their robes and made them white in the
blood (i.e. the death) of the Lamb (i.e. Jesus, willingly
sacrificed for them).' A rescue operation indeed. Where else in
the religions of the world do you hear of a God who undertakes
salvation for his people by personally bearing responsibility for
their wickedness and allowing it to crush him?

But even that is not all. The God who has revealed himself
and rescued us has done it for a purpose. Amazingly, he wants
to relate to us. That is where the resurrection comes in. He is no
dead figure in a history book, two thousand years out of date.
He is alive, and we can have dealings with him. I remember
vividly the day when this truth became a reality to me. I asked

the Risen One to come and live in me. He has done so. I have not found God. I could not if I wanted to, and I would not have wanted to anyway, so self-centred was I. But he has found me. He came to earth to reveal himself to me. He died to remove the beastliness of my wrongdoing. He lives, and is at work changing my life from the inside. And all this I find to be very good news.

No other faith does anything remotely like this. No other faith claims to. Christianity is quite distinct from other religions. It is not a case of man in search of God but of God in search of man. Not a religion at all, but a revelation and a rescue.

It is at this point that two important questions arise.

'IF YOU ARE RIGHT ABOUT JESUS, ARE OTHER RELIGIONS ALL WRONG?'

By no means. The God who made the world, the God who revealed himself in Christ, has not left himself without witness in the world. Every good thought, every gleam of light, every word of truth to be found in any religion, and in atheistic philosophies like Marxism as well, is part of God's self-disclosure. All truth is God's truth, and has its focus in the one who became incarnate. So Christians welcome truth wherever it is found. As you look into other faiths you will find an enormous amount that is true and worthy, that is moral and good, as well as much that is not. But you will not find anything that is good and true which cannot be found in Christ. You will not hear from them about a God who cares for you enough to die for you, to rise from the grave as a pledge of your future, and to be willing to come and share your life with you. You will not find in any other faith a revelation of God in fully personal terms, a rescue of man from his self-centredness and sin, and the offer by this God to come and indwell the life of every man, woman or child who welcomes him.

It is not that Christians are narrow-minded about other faiths. But if Jesus is, as the resurrection asserts, God himself come to our rescue, then it is crass folly to reject him. And this is something that we can investigate for ourselves. We are not dealing with myth and legend, such as makes it impossible to know when Buddha lived (estimates vary between 1000 and 500 B.C.) or details of his birth (there are 547 birth stories). We are dealing with history. Christians claim (and there is plenty of documentary evidence to support the claim) that Jesus of Nazareth rose from the dead on the first Easter Day in A.D. 30 or 31 and launched the Christian community. His scattered followers did not expect it. To begin with they did not believe it. But they were driven to do so by their experience of the risen Jesus, and once they were convinced, nothing could silence them. For they had discovered the key to life. They did not claim merely that a corpse has been resuscitated. That would not have done much good. They believed that Almighty God took our nature as the man Jesus, that he suffered and died, *and that death could not hold him*! His resurrection says 'Yes' to his claim to be the Way, the Truth and the Life. The resurrection vindicates his claim to deity. In the risen Jesus God confronts us with shattering directness. He offers us total aid; but he demands of us total obedience. It is splendid to have an interest in comparative religion. But the more you know of others the more you see Christianity to be unique. And the key to Christianity is the resurrection.

I have investigated the reliability of the resurrection with some care in a little book *Man Alive*, and we shall be looking at the evidence more briefly in Chapter 9. But the point is this. Christianity is a historical religion. It claims that God has taken the risk of involving himself in human history, and the evidence is there for you to examine with the utmost rigour. The facts will stand any amount of critical examination. No book on earth has been subjected to such prolonged and detailed scrutiny by some of the best minds in the world over many hundreds of years as the New Testament. Examine the evidence for yourself, and do not rely on second hand opinions from those who believe the Christian story or from those who reject it. This is the most important issue you will ever have to decide. Did Jesus rise from the dead or not? If not, then there will be time enough to look to all the other faiths in the world, to see what help for living can be found in them. But if he did rise, and you are persuaded of it, then that settles for you the question of which religion. Christ can no longer appear to you just as a very fine man. Although fully human he somehow brings God to you. And as God he claims your loyal obedience.

The second question that commonly arises at this point is this.

'IF YOU ARE RIGHT ABOUT JESUS, ARE ALL NON-CHRISTIANS INEVITABLY LOST?'

Here again the answer is No. It is certainly not taught in the New Testament that all who have not heard of Jesus Christ are inevitably lost. The whole Bible makes it plain that men will be judged by God with utter fairness and they will be judged by their response to such light as they have had. In a famous passage of his Letter to the Romans Paul maintains resolutely that God has no favourites. 'When Gentiles who do not have the Law do by nature what the Law requires, they constitute a law over against themselves (even though they do not have the Law). They show that what the Law requires is written on their hearts, while their conscience also bears witness and their conflicting thoughts either accuse or perhaps excuse them, on that day when God judges the secrets of men by Jesus Christ' (Romans 2: 14, 15). He means that heathen nations who do not have God's revelation in the Scriptures still have a knowledge of right and wrong; their moral sense acts as law-giver and judge within them, and either commends or condemns them for what they do. God is absolutely fair. But Paul goes on to show that this breath of opportunity does not much help. For pagan and Jew alike have failed to keep God's holy law, or even their own relative standards, the inner law of conscience. No man, therefore, can be reconciled with God on the grounds of his own goodness and sincerity; for no man's goodness and sincerity are perfect — far from it, in fact. Paul's solemn conclusion of that whole passage in the first three chapters of Romans, where he surveys the moral records of religious and pagan world alike, is this: 'every mouth shall be stopped, and all the world shall be found guilty before God' (3: 19). And that is the backcloth against which he sets forth the joyful news that what no man can do for himself, or for anyone else, God has done for all who will trust him, be they religious or pagan by background. He has made it possible for us to be accepted in his beloved Son, Jesus Christ.

Christ died 'not for our sins only', says the New Testament, 'but for the sins of the whole world'. He died so that men of faith in Old Testament days could have their accusing record wiped clean. Now Abraham and the others did not know how God would find it possible to accept sinful men like themselves. They just trusted him when he made it clear to them that they were accepted. We, with our greater perspective, know that Abraham was saved because of what God in Christ was going to do for him on that cross of Calvary. It would seem consistent, therefore, with God's gracious activity, that those who have not heard of Christ in centuries since Calvary could also wake up on the other side of death to find themselves accepted with God, if they have really repented of their sins and cast themselves upon the mercy of God. For did not Jesus teach us that his heavenly Father is accustomed to give to everyone who asks, and to open the door to everyone who asks? The condition of asking, of seeking, of knocking, of repenting in self-abandonment and despair at our own goodness — that is the human side. But God's side has been made plain at the cross. He is prepared to accept any man of any tribe at any time into his heavenly kingdom.

It has sometimes been thought that to admit this would be to cut the nerve of missionary endeavour. But this is not the case. Many a missionary has gone to a place where the gospel has never been preached. He has spoken of the love of God for sinners. The response from one or two of his hearers, but by no means all of them, has been to say, 'We have been looking for something like this all our lives. We gladly repent and surrender our lives to the God who has so loved us. But, oh, why did you not come and tell us this before?'

It has sometimes been thought that to admit this 'wider hope' is to let us off the hook of deciding for Christ or against him. But nothing could be further from the truth. The heathen in a pagan land, who repents and believes the first time he hears the gospel, has been searching for years. He is in a very different situation from the careless Western churchgoer who says, 'What about all those who have never heard the gospel? Surely all religions lead to God?' in order to avoid commitment of any sort. Such a man is frivolous. He has no excuse for rejecting the Light of the world, Jesus. For the evidence lies open to him in the Scriptures, which he can buy for a few pence. He is surrounded by Christian believers who know from first hand the experience the truth of what is written in those Scriptures. He is without excuse if he does not follow the lead of the Scriptures and the men who have found the truth, in coming to Jesus in the surrender of faith and obedience.

There is one category of people who, the New Testament tells us, will be lost. It is not those who have never heard. It is those who have heard and said 'No'. Such were many of the Pharisees in the time of Jesus. He sadly had to say of them, 'You search the Scriptures, because you think that in them you have eternal life. But you would not come to me that you might have life.' And when in his second letter to the Christians at Thessalonica Paul speaks of the possibility of hell, he does so in the terrifyingly simple terms of 'everlasting destruction from the presence of the Lord', and he asserts, following his Master, that it awaits those who, having heard the good news of God's rescue, 'obey not the gospel of our Lord Jesus Christ' (2 Thessalonians 1:9). Let us make sure we do not belong to their number.

5

'Jesus was just a good man'

OURS IS A questing generation. We won't take anything on authority, and if an opinion is old it is probably wrong! We want instant truth, instant relevance. Old dogmas such as the Church's view that Jesus of Nazareth was divine simply don't turn us on any more. And yet we remain fascinated by Jesus. Books about him continue to pour from the presses despite the soaring cost of paper and printing. Films about him are box office successes. Rock operas such as *Jesus Christ Superstar* and

Godspell get top world ratings. He certainly has not lost his appeal. But we aren't quite sure what to make of him.

David Essex, who played Jesus in *Godspell,* was asked why he thought there was such a vogue for religious musicals. Did it say anything about us as a generation? He replied, 'I think it does. We all went through a period of trying to find a complete mystic experience. Lots of people tried drugs and lots of people tried Eastern religions. Then we found that that didn't work, so consequently we went back to Christianity, but in a kind of new way. We identified in Jesus a *different* kind of man, a kind of Che Guevara figure, if you like, that wasn't political.'

I find that helpful. Jesus was, on any showing, a great man, a good man, a fabulous teacher, heroically dedicated. But so have others been. David Essex begins to put his finger on that special quality about Jesus when he says 'a different kind of man'. Let's get back to the New Testament documents and look a bit closer at that difference — and then see whether the easy solution 'Jesus was just a good man' will carry conviction or not.

1. His character was different

Different from any man who ever lived. That character has dominated the world in the two thousand years since he walked the narrow streets of Nazareth. To be sure, Mohammed has had profound influence, and so has Socrates. But nothing like Jesus. Jesus has captured the heart and mind and allegiance of peasant and king, of intellectual and illiterate the world over, all down the centuries. It makes no difference whether you go to the Naga tribesmen in the hill country of India, or the warlike Masai in Kenya, black and white in Southern Africa and the U.S.A., the men of Fiji and of Finland, of Singapore and Sebastapol. Everywhere there are Christians. Wherever the message of this man Jesus has been proclaimed, some men of every tribe and culture and background and intellect have turned from their own ways to follow him. This has brought opposition, often persecution. It has meant self-sacrifice and ostracism. But that has not stopped people succumbing to the spell of Jesus.

You could, I suppose, say the same of Lenin or Mao. At least, nearly the same. They have a tremendous following in certain parts of the world. Their followers have often gained in material prosperity, in living standards, and in a goal to live for. But the appeal has been to one class of person only. Mao brings hope to the oppressed worker, but offers nothing but doom to the bourgeois. Jesus too offers hope, justice, and love to the poor, but he also reaches the rich and disillusioned. He changes them, to be sure; but he does not threaten them or require of them the rejection of their class. Moreover the philosophy behind a Lenin or a Mao has a lot of envy and hate about it, a lot of ruthlessness in the pursuit of ideology, and a terrifying indifference to truth. Where do you find, in the whole history of mankind, a character that has dominated and appealed to men of every generation and type, and in so doing has transformed them for the better? Nowhere but Jesus. That one solitary life is without parallel. Do you know that anonymous piece entitled 'One Solitary Life'? Here it is:

He was born in an obscure village, the child of a peasant woman.

He grew up in still another village, where he worked in a carpenter's shop till he was thirty. Then for three years he was an itinerant preacher.

He never wrote a book. He never held an office. He never had a family or owned a house. He didn't go to college. He never visited a big city. He never travelled two hundred miles from the place where he was born. He did none of the things one usually associates with greatness.

He had no credentials but himself.

He was only thirty-three when the tide of public opinion turned against him. His friends ran away. He was turned over to his enemies and went through the mockery of a trial. He was nailed to a cross between two thieves. While he was dying, his executioners gambled for his clothing, the only property he had on earth. When he was dead he was laid in a borrowed grave through the pity of a friend.

Nineteen centuries have come and gone, and today he is the central figure of the human race and the leader of mankind's progress. All the armies that ever marched, all the navies that ever sailed, all the parliaments that ever sat, all the kings that ever reigned, put together, have not affected the life of man on this earth as much as that ONE SOLITARY LIFE.

If Jesus was just a good man, I wonder what it was that made his life so different? David Essex called him 'a kind of Che Guevara figure that wasn't political'. Che is a marvellous parallel ... and contrast. Son of a rich family, himself a highly educated banker and doctor, he gave himself to the cause of the underprivileged in Bolivia. Like Jesus before him, 'though he was rich, yet for your sakes he became poor ...' Like Jesus, he led a movement of radical opposition to the corrupt existing regime. Like Jesus, he was betrayed and killed. Like Jesus, he evoked the admiration and dedication of a worldwide band of followers. But there the similarity ends. Unlike Che, Jesus did not preach or practise hatred and violence against his foes: rather, love. Unlike Che, he did not take up arms. Unlike Che, he was not tricked to his death, but went to it in the dignity of a voluntary choice. Unlike Che, he does not remain dead and gone, with nothing but his memory and ideals to cheer his followers. For Jesus lives, as we shall see in Chapter 9, and it is highly significant that in the past couple of years or so there has broken out a Christian revival in Bolivia, in which over 60,000 people have turned from the shadow to the reality, from Che Guevara to Christ. There is, you see, something different about him.

2. HIS TEACHING WAS DIFFERENT

Nobody ever taught like this. That was the conclusion of the soldiers sent to arrest him. St. John tells us that when the Pharisees asked them why they had not obeyed orders, they replied 'No man ever spoke like this man' (John 7: 46). He taught them, says the earliest evangelist, as one who had authority, and not like the teachers of the day. These men would prop up their opinions by endless references to teachers before them who had held the same view — rather like the acres of footnotes in modern scholarly books about God. Jesus prefaced his teaching with the remarkable formula, unknown in all literature, 'Truly, truly I say to you.' Who was this 'I' who spoke with such authority? Who was this man who spoke so much about the Kingdom of God, and calmly announced that he was bringing it in? 'Until John, it was the law and the prophets,' he once said. 'Since then, it is the good news of the Kingdom of God.' In other words, his forerunner, John the Baptist, marked the end of the old era: he inaugurated the new. This accounts for the note of urgency which runs through those remarkable parables of his. The farmer who has been sowing and tending his seed now has to harvest the crop: if he lets the moment pass, the crop is lost. The pearl fancier who finds the best pearl he has ever seen, or the ploughman who turns up a bag of buried treasure in a field — for both zero hour has arrived: they must go for it even if it means gambling their whole capital. The generous householder has spread his banquet and invited all and sundry; to make excuses at this juncture, to refuse the invitation would be disastrous — it would mean final exclusion from the party. No wonder that the whole countryside was agog at teaching like this. There was nothing comparable in the religious history of the world.

You only had to compare Jesus' teaching with the Old Testament to get the message. Now, don't get me wrong. Jesus took the Old Testament as his Bible. He believed that it was inspired by God, and was therefore decisive both for himself and his hearers. But still he can contrast his teaching with it, not as black against white, but as fulfilment over against promise. 'I have not come to abolish the law and the prophets, but to fulfil,' he claimed (Matthew 5: 17). And he proceeded to show what he meant. 'Your goodness has to be better than that of the

religious leaders,' he maintained — and explained that many
religious men make a show of their piety in order to impress
men; they give to be praised by men; and they pray to be seen
by men. Secret prayer, unseen generosity, unostentatious religion is the order of the day for the follower of Jesus.

Or take the matter of murder. 'You have heard that it was
said to the men of old, "You shall not kill; and whoever kills
shall be liable to judgment." But I say to you that everyone who
is angry with his brother without cause shall be liable to judgment' (Matthew 5: 21). Jesus is not abolishing the Old Testament law of manslaughter. He is fulfilling the principle
behind it, for he is showing how God hates the evil thought of
uncontrolled fury no less than the bitter outcome in murder.
Again, he takes the famous maxim from the Old Testament,
'An eye for an eye and a tooth for a tooth' and adds, 'But I say
to you, "Do not resist one who is evil." ' (Matthew 5: 38). Is he
repudiating the Old Testament principle? Not at all. He per-
ceives the principle that lay behind it (that of limiting revenge
to the equivalent of the wrong done) and fulfils that principle
by allowing love to banish revenge altogether.

This matter of love was hard enough to fulfil, even to the
folk you liked. So the Old Testament had said, 'You shall love
your neighbour,' and to it the scribes had enthusiastically added
what the Old Testament did not add, 'and hate your enemy'!
To this Jesus brings an undreamed-of fulfilment, a new thing in
the history of thought, an ethic which is the most difficult and
the most powerful in today's world as it was then: 'But I say to
you, Love your enemies, and pray for those who persecute you,
just as your heavenly Father does' (Matthew 5: 43).

If you want more of this, turn to the Sermon on the Mount in
Matthew chs. 5–7. But the point is clear enough. Though Jesus
built on God's revelation in the Old Testament, he taught a
fulfilment of what had been foreshadowed there which was
breathtakingly new, completely lucid, intensely profound, and
as relevant now as it was then.

Now I ask you. Where can you find anything in the teaching
of Jesus that does not strike you as truth? Where can you find

anything that strikes you as error? How do you account for the fact that no ethical advances, no teaching of how men should behave towards their fellows has emerged in the centuries since then which represent any advance on the Man of Nazareth? Where did the man get this fantastic teaching from? He had an answer: 'My teaching is not mine, but His that sent me' (John 7: 16). Could he be right? Did he come from God? Could this account at one fell swoop for his authority, his simplicity, his depth, his world-wide appeal? If you reply, 'Of course not: he was just a very impressive teacher,' I want to ask you a question or two.

Why did he strike contemporaries and subsequent generations as so utterly different from other teachers? How is it that he got all this learning without having been to college? How is it that, unlike other great teachers such as Socrates and Mohammed, his teaching fits all men everywhere? How is it that nobody has dreamed up any moral advances since his teaching? What was there in his heredity and his environment to account for this unique teacher, and the remarkable fact that no greater has ever looked like emerging? Yes, there was something different about this teacher. Perhaps it was not so strange when he took over the old Jewish saying 'When two or three busy themselves over the Law of God, the glory of God shines upon them' and replaced it with 'Where two or three are gathered together in my name, there am I in their midst' (Matthew 18: 20). Perhaps he *was* different.

3. His behaviour was different

Time and again he told doubters not to believe him unless his behaviour bore him out. His works, as he sometimes called them, had to match his words. And they did. Exactly. How sublime to be able to tell the story of the shepherd who goes out at night and braves danger to seek one lost sheep — and carries on until he finds it. But more sublime still to go and live it out by loving a Simon Peter even when he denied knowing him, and deserted him in his moment of greatest need. It is marvellous to find Jesus talking of the love his Father has for all men irrespective of their merits; love which, like the rain and sunshine, falls on all alike. It is even more marvellous to give the favourite's portion at a supper party to the man you know is just about to betray you, and then to kiss him on the cheek as he does so! It is one thing to say 'Blessed are the poor', and quite another to be happy in poverty, as Jesus was. One thing to say 'Bless your enemies', and quite another matter to cry 'Father, forgive them' as cruel soldiers nail your bleeding body to a cross. But that is the way Jesus behaved. His actions matched his teaching.

That is something that has never been equalled. Socrates, Plato, Moses, Confucius, and in our own day Martin Luther King, Pope John, or Billy Graham taught wonderful things and men have hung on their words. But never did any of these great men actually manage to carry out all they taught. In all of them there has been consciousness of failure. Indeed, this is one of the surest marks of greatness — to recognise that one's object exceeds one's reach, the goal lies far beyond the achievement. And growth in greatness always carries with it growth in humility. Talk to any truly great individual, and he will tell you how ashamed he is of his failures and of his mistakes. The most famous saints are always most conscious of wrong within.

But Jesus was different. He taught the highest standards that any teacher has formulated, and he kept them. He really did. There is remarkable unanimity on this matter. It is interesting to note how united the opposition to Jesus is about his innocence. Three times in the account of the trial before Pilate, the governor pronounces his innocence. Pilate's wife sends a message to the courtroom to the same effect. The Jewish leaders cannot find an accusation which will stick, and so they have to get him to incriminate himself by admitting to be the Messiah. Even the traitor Judas confesses that he has betrayed innocent blood. Even the brigands crucified with him recognised that he had done nothing wrong. Even the man in charge of the crucifixion was driven to exclaim, 'This man was innocent.'

Quite an impressive bunch of testimony from the Opposition benches. Jesus was different.

Perhaps still more impressive is the testimony of his friends. The more we know someone, the less inclined we are to entertain any exaggerated claim on their behalf: we know them too well. But not in Jesus' case. John knew him intimately. Yet he could call Jesus 'the true Light which gives light to every man', and could assert, 'If we say we have no sin we deceive ourselves ... but in him there is no sin.' Peter could call him 'the just one' in contrast to us 'the unjust', and could be so overcome by the quality of Jesus' life that he fell at his feet on one occasion and asked him to depart from a sinner like himself. Paul calls Jesus the sinless one; the writer to the Hebrews spoke of him as just the one we need, 'holy, blameless, unstained, separate from sinners'. In short, every strand of the New Testament, written as it was by those who knew Jesus or knew of him well, is quite clear on this matter: his life was perfect. It was a moral miracle. His life was different from other men's, and showed theirs up.

This is precisely what we seem to find in Jesus' own allusions to his behaviour. We never find him having to apologise. We never find him having to admit he was wrong. And this from the man who was so shrewd in spotting hypocrisy in others! There are several occasions when we are given the substance of his prayers; but never once do they betray any shadow of consciousness of guilt. He tells us to pray 'Forgive us our trespasses', but significantly he does not seem to need to do so himself. Fascinating. Unique. Here is a person of the most refined spiritual insight who can say of his heavenly Father, 'I do always those things that please him' (John 8: 29). Here is a man who can turn to an angry crowd furious because he was claiming that he was one with God, and with childlike innocence can ask them, 'Which of you can convict me of sin?' (John 8: 46). I do not know which is the more remarkable: that he could ask such a question — or that he could not be faulted by the crowd!

Whichever way you look at it, that life was unique. He alone of all the people known to history has come down to us with a clean sheet. No mud slung at him has stuck. His behaviour was blameless. What other man has behaved like that? Even for one day? Very well then, will it do simply to say 'Jesus was no more than a fine teacher'? Isn't that a very shallow assumption, in the light of a life that was so staggeringly different?

4. HIS ABILITIES WERE DIFFERENT

You cannot disentangle Jesus from miracle. Scholars in the last century spent endless ingenuity on the quest of a non-miraculous Jesus. In the end it was an acknowledged failure. Because every strand in the evidence about Jesus shows him as different from other men: through him God acted in a way impossible to understand on the assumption that he was just a good man. The miracles begin at his birth: he was God's Son, according to Mark; God's Word and agent in creation, according to John; the full repository of the Godhead according to Paul (whilst none the less being 'born of a woman'); the one who came into the world without the agency of a human father, according to Matthew and Luke. The miracles continue in his ministry: miracles of healing, or exorcism, nature miracles (such as the feeding of the multitude from a handful of loaves, and his walking on the sea in a storm), and supremely his raising from the dead Lazarus, the widow of Nain's son, and Jairus' daughter. Last of all came the greatest of all miracles, his own resurrection from the grave — not just to a further span of life but to a new quality of life over which death has no power. Such is the testimony of the New Testament: a Jesus who was different, in view of the powers at his command. In the first three Gospels these miracles are actually called 'acts of power' in the original Greek. But St. John's Gospel shows the true significance of the miracles when he calls them 'signs'. Signs of who Jesus is. Signs of what he can do for men. The one who fed a multitide can feed the hungry soul. The one who opened blind eyes can do the same for men blinded by pride and prejudice. The one who raised the dead can bring new life to someone who is dead spiritually and morally. The miracles were never done for selfish purposes; never to show off. They were evoked by Jesus' compassion for human need, and they were intended both to show that the long awaited Messianic kingdom had begun, and also that Jesus was the liberator who could unlock the various chains of man.

It is fashionable to laugh at the miracles. Such things could not happen. But why not? The laws of nature do not forbid them. A 'law of nature' is simply the name we give to a series of observed uniformities; this is the way things happen. But if a contrary instance is well attested, the scientist will widen his so-called 'law' to embrace both the uniformities and the exception to the rule. In the case of Jesus there is lots of strong contemporary evidence that he was the exception to the rule. If he was just a good man, that would be astonishing, perhaps meaningless. If he was different, if he was in some way God himself coming to disclose himself to us within the limitations of human form — then perhaps it is neither so incredible nor so meaningless that he should perform miracles.

At all events the evidence is overwhelming, and it is not all contained within the pages of the New Testament. You will find the earliest Christian apologist, a man called Quadratus, writing early in the second century:

> But the works of our Saviour were always present (for they were genuine): namely those who were healed, those who rose from the dead. They were not only seen in the act of being healed or raised, but they remained always present. And not merely when the Saviour was on earth, but after his departure as well. They lived on for a considerable time, so much so that some of them have survived even to our own day.

I find it intriguing that this, the only passage of Quadratus to have survived, should be devoted to drawing out the implications and establishing the truth of the miracles. It shows how confidently the early Christians could look to the miracles of Jesus as a pointer to his being more than man, to his being different.

But there are traces of his miracles in Roman and Jewish sources as well. Justin Martyr, writing his *Apology* about A.D. 150, can say with casual confidence, 'That he performed these miracles you may easily satisfy yourself from the *Acts* of Pontius Pilate.' It was the same with the Jews. We find them in the Gospels unable to deny the miracles of Jesus, but taking the only way out — attributing them to the devil. In the Acts of the Apostles we find Jews attempting to use the name of Jesus as a potent spell in exorcism: later on this continued, so much so that the writers in the *Mishnah* (Jewish law code) have to forbid Jews to heal in the name of Jesus! And the Tractate *Sanhedrin* tells us that Jesus 'was hanged on the eve of the Passover because he practised sorcery and led Israel astray' — a plain reference to his miracles.

Clearly, this man was different . . .

5. HIS FULFILMENT OF SCRIPTURE WAS DIFFERENT

Strikingly different. It hit the first disciples between the eyes. So much so that they found themselves writing like this: 'this was done in order to fulfil the words of the prophet Isaiah . . .' and the like. It is a recurring theme in the New Testament. Now this is very remarkable. The first followers of Jesus, being Jews, had the highest reverence for the Scriptures of the Old Testament. Yet there were manifestly incomplete sides to them. Those Scriptures spoke of a day when God would judge the earth. They spoke of a king of David's stock whose dominion would be endless. They spoke of all the families of man being blessed in Abraham, the man of faith who had started the nation of Israel. They spoke of one like a Son of Man coming to the Ancient of Days, and receiving a kingdom that would never be destroyed, together with power, glory and judgment. They spoke of a prophet like Moses arising among the people whose teaching would be unparalleled. They spoke of a Servant of the Lord whose suffering would be intense and whose death would carry away the sins of the people. They spoke of a Son of God whose character would measure up to that of his Father. This coming one would fulfil the role of prophet, of priest and of king for ever. He would be born of David's lineage, but of a humble, despised family. His birthplace would be Bethlehem. He would both restore the fallen in Israel and be a light to the Gentiles. He would be despised and rejected by the very people he came to rescue from their self-centredness. He would die among malefactors, and his tomb would be supplied by a rich man. But that would not be the end of him. He would live again, and the Lord's programme would prosper in his hands. When he saw all that would be accomplished by the anguish of his soul, he would be satisfied. For he would have forged a new agreement between God and man by his death; indeed, his death would open up the possibility of ordinary men and women having the Spirit of God come and take up residence within their lives.

All of this came true with Jesus. Not some of it: all of it. There is no example in the literature of the whole world where the prophecies made centuries beforehand in a holy book were fulfilled in a historical person in this way. It amazed his followers, but it convinced them. They came to see in him, the humble carpenter of Nazareth, the fulfilment of these ancient prophecies. He was born in Bethlehem of David's stock. His teaching showed him to be the prophet like Moses. He was the Suffering Servant of the Lord whose anguish on the cross brought pardon for all who would believe, as Abraham had believed. He was the one who would restore the fortunes of Israel and open the way of faith up to the Gentiles. He had established this new covenant between God and man, sealing it with his blood. His death had made the ultimate sacrifice, and no priesthood was ever to be needed again — for he had once and for all reconciled men to God by his own self-offering. His kingly rule would be for ever; veiled now, but apparent when he came to judge. His Spirit was already at work in the transformed lives of the disciples.

In the centuries that followed, this argument from prophecy

had an enormous impact. Many distinguished pagans were won to faith in Jesus by the way he fulfilled the prophecies made in these writings of an Old Testament which seemed so much older and so much nobler than their own writings of Homer and Plato. And many still are. As Professor Moule, one of the leading New Testament scholars in England, puts it:

The notion of the 'fulfilment' of Scripture in a single individual, a figure of recent history, and he a condemned and disgraced criminal, who claimed to be the coping stone of the whole structure, and the goal of God's whole design, was new. And it was the Christian community which first related together, round a single focus, the scattered and largely disconnected images of Israel's hope. It was utterly new for images like 'Messiah', 'Christ', 'Son of God', 'Son of Man', 'Suffering Servant' and 'Lord' to be seen as inter-changeable terms all relating to one figure (*The Phenomenon of the New Testament*, p. 16).

That figure *was* different.

So different that we find the New Testament writers attributing to him titles and activities reserved for God himself in the Old Testament. For instance, in Isaiah (41: 4, 44: 6, 48: 12) God calls himself 'the First and the Last', but in the New Testament this title is applied to Jesus (Revelation 1: 11, 2: 8, 22: 13). 'I am' is the special name of God (Yahweh, usually known as Jehovah) and it is too sacred to be pronounced, so that the Jews used the word Adonai, Lord, as a substitute. But we find claims to be the 'I am' coming on the lips of Jesus; notably the fantastic claim of John 8: 58, 'Before Abraham was, I am.' So much so that when asked, at a crucial stage in his trial, whether he was the Messiah, Jesus replied, 'I am, and you shall see the Son of Man sitting at the right hand of power and coming with the clouds of heaven' (Mark 14: 62.) This produced so savage a reaction in the high priest and his colleagues because it appeared to be a claim to personal deity on the part of Jesus.

Again, who is it in the Old Testament who is the Shepherd of his people? God, of course. 'The Lord is my Shepherd,' begins that most famous Psalm 23. But Jesus calmly uses the title of himself, 'I am the good Shepherd'; and other New Testament writers such as Peter and the writer to the Hebrews speak of him as 'the chief shepherd' and 'the great shepherd'. They had got the message. Perhaps the most remarkable function of God in the Old Testament was to create the world. 'In the beginning, God created the heaven and the earth' is, after all the opening sentence of the whole Bible. But listen to Paul: 'By Christ were all things created in the heavens and upon earth . . . all things have been created through him and for him' (Colossians 1: 16). Listen to John: 'He was in the beginning with God: all things were made through him, and without him was not anything made that was made' (John 1: 3).

Clearly, this man was different. No good man fulfilled all the strands of ancient scriptures, themselves penned over a thousand years, as this man did. Perhaps his contemporaries were right in believing he was one with God.

6. HIS CLAIMS WERE DIFFERENT

If you have read the Gospels, you may well have been struck by a remarkable contrast. On the one hand Jesus is a humble, self-forgetful figure, healing the sick, teaching the people, befriending the outcast. He is no academic theologian, but a horny-handed carpenter whose words are full of hard-headed wisdom and earthy illustrations. He has no money, no settled home, no vote, no rights. On the other hand he makes the most fantastic claims, and many of them are almost casual, throw-away remarks. For example, he takes it for granted that he is entitled to man's worship, the worship due to God alone. When Peter falls at his feet in adoration after a fishing expedition and says, 'Depart from me, for I am a sinful man, master' (Luke 5: 8), Jesus does nothing to stop him. When Thomas falls at his feet after the resurrection and exclaims, 'My Lord and my God' (John 20: 28), Jesus does not rebuke him — except for needing the evidence of his eyes to come to that conclusion. No good man would do that. Indeed we have examples in the New Testament of two good men, Peter and Paul, who found themselves being worshipped by ignorant pagans, and they reacted violently against it, telling them to worship God alone. Jesus seems to have taken such worship as his due.

Watch him deal with a woman taken in adultery, or a man sick with paralysis (John 8: 1ff, Mark 2: 1ff). 'Your sins are forgiven you,' says Jesus, and in the case of the paralytic he gave a visual demonstration of the fact — the man got up at Jesus' command and walked! Now what are we to make of a claim like that? The Pharisees knew very well what to make of it. 'Who is this that forgives sins?' they asked. 'There is one who forgives sins, God.' That is precisely the point. Jesus was laying implicit claim to do what God does, to forgive men their sins. Indeed, when Mary is told that her baby must be called Jesus, the explanation of the name is brought out like this: 'for he shall save his people from their sins'. In the Old Testament (Psalm 130: 8) this task for forgiving sins is specially, and naturally, said to belong to God alone. Here, right at the start of his life, Jesus takes on the job. The implication is obvious. In Jesus we meet someone who is different. He is no merely good man.

What are we to make of this? C. S. Lewis puts the challenge with his customary force.

There is no halfway house, and there is no parallel in other religions. If you had gone to Buddha and asked him: 'Are you the son of Bramah?' he would have said, 'My son, you are still in the vale of illusion.' If you had gone to Socrates and asked, 'Are you Zeus?' he would have laughed at you. If you had gone to Mohammed and asked, 'Are you Allah?' he would first have rent his clothes and then cut off your head. If you had asked Confucius, 'Are you heaven?' I think he would probably have replied, 'Remarks which are not in accordance with nature are in bad taste.'

This man was different. He was no merely great teacher.
Listen to Lewis once again:

The things he says are very different from what any other
teacher has said. Others say, 'This is the truth about the
universe. This is the way you ought to go.' But he says, 'I am
the Truth and the Way and the Life.' He says, 'No man can
reach absolute reality, except through me. Try to retain your
own life and you will inevitably be ruined. Give yourself
away and you will be saved.' He says, 'If you are ashamed of
me, if, when you hear my call you turn the other way, I will
look the other way when I come again as God without dis-
guise. If anything whatever is keeping you from God and
from me, whatever it is, throw it away. If it is your eye, pull
it out. If it is your hand, cut it off. If you put yourself first
you will be last. Come to me, everyone who is carrying a
heavy load, and I will set that right. Your sins, all of them,
are wiped out. I can do that. I am Re-birth, I am Life. Eat
me, drink me, I am your food. And finally, do not be afraid, I
have overcome the whole universe.' That is the issue.

Yes, that is the issue. What are you going to make of it? In
the light of his character and teaching, his behaviour and miracles, his fulfilment of prophecy and his astonishing claims,
what are you going to say? He backed the whole thing up with a
death such as the world has never seen, and, unlike any other
person before or since, a resurrection from the grave. (I shall
deal with his cross in chapter 8 and his resurrection in chapter
9.) It was the way he died and the way he rose that supremely
convinced the first disciples that the man Jesus was nothing less
than God. 'He was declared to be Son of God, powerfully,
through the resurrection from the dead,' wrote Saul or Tarsus,
once such a doughty opponent of the Christian faith, but now
convinced by that death and resurrection that Jesus' claims
were true.

Take a long, cool, look at the evidence I have brought before
you in this chapter. Read any one of the Gospels with an open,

enquiring mind. And then if you still say, 'Jesus was just a good man,' I shall say, 'You must be joking.' That is the one thing he cannot be. That is the one thing the men on the spot never thought of calling him. They were terrified of him: they believed him: or they hounded him to death. But nobody patronisingly said of him, 'What a splendid preacher we had in the synagogue last Sabbath. You must come along and hear him some time.' Jesus does not present himself to us as the best example of the human race, for our edification. He comes to us from beyond the human race, as God himself, hastening to our rescue. He expects of us, indeed demands of us, not our admiration but our allegiance, not our patronage but our hearts. He has the rights of God Almighty over us. And he can make all the difference of God Almighty within us, once we allow room for him in the lives he has given us.

Do you know Gordon Bailey's poem *The Lord Jesus Christ*? This is what he wrote after he had made room for Christ in his life:

> When he said
> 'I am the Way'
> he was claiming
> that only he could lead
> man to God.
>
> When he said
> 'I am the Truth'
> he was claiming
> universal and exclusive rights
> on the ability to reveal
> God to man.
>
> When he said
> 'I am the Life'
> he was claiming
> to be that quality of existence
> sacrificed for and sought by
> men and gods.

He also claimed
a supernatural birth,
an impossible death, and
a miraculous resurrection.

His claims mean that he is either
utterly insane,
undeniably evil, or
uniquely everything he claims to be!

6

'It doesn't matter what you believe so long as you are sincere'

ATTRACTIVE, BUT WRONG

Lots of people seem to believe this. And it is certainly a very attractive position to hold. For one thing it is eminently tolerant; and tolerance is just about the only virtue that has escaped the corroding cynicism of our day. It sounds a very liberal and enlightened creed, for it means that everyone will win the race; everyone will get prizes.

There is another reason for its appeal. At a stroke it removes the problem of seeking the truth, the embarrassment of being challenged by it. And that is very agreeable. After all, we are so busy these days we have little time to examine the different religions of the world, and we have no desire to have our lives unmasked by the truth when we find it.

What is more, this view that it doesn't matter what you believe so long as you are sincere has the great advantage of giving voice to our deep-seated disgust at insincerity. It is always a blow when a man or a country loudly professes one thing and then promptly does another. A classic example of this insincerity was given not so long ago by Haile Selasse, Emperor of Ethiopia, who claimed the most ancient continuous empire in the world. Temporarily deposed when the Italians invaded Ethiopia in 1935, he was restored in 1941 partly through the good offices of the South African Government. In gratitude, he vowed eternal friendship to them — and subsequently founded the Organisation for African Unity, one of whose prime targets many consider has been the destruction of the existing structures in South Africa! He professed to be a liberator of his people, but two thirds of the population were kept in serfdom. He claimed to uphold justice and fair play, but he and a small nobility retained most of the best land in the country. For all his professed love of his people, he was content to ship enormous loads of Ethiopian gold overseas, while hundreds of thousands of his countrymen die of starvation and cholera. The man was insincere. And he was toppled from power. We cannot help feeling that this was right and proper. 'He had it coming to him,' we say, because sincerity is very important, and no matter how broadminded we are, we cannot stand a man who is two-faced.

Insincerity is bad in individuals. It is worse in a whole country. I heard on the radio, the morning I wrote this chapter, some extracts from the South African Ambassador, Mr. Pik Botha's speech to the United Nations when he was seeking to avoid South Africa's expulsion from the world body. He claimed that his country did not discriminate against a man simply on the grounds of his colour. The effrontery of such a claim, the sheer insincerity of it, is breathtaking to one who, as I was at the time, lives in South Africa and sees daily the discrimination all around him. But what about the African nations which were hounding South Africa for racialism at the United Nations? Is there no racial discrimination in Kenya between the Kikuyu and the Luo? Or in Burundi as the Tutsi slaughter the Hutu? Or in Uganda where the Asians were unceremoniously bundled out of the country simply and solely because of the colour of their skin? Insincerity stinks wherever it is found.

But perhaps the worst kind of insincerity is the religious sort. The corruption of the Czarist church in ninteenth century Russia, or of the Coptic church in Ethiopia today is positively sickening. In the last century in England thousands of working men went to church in order to keep in with the bosses, not because they were believing Christians. We have no time for insincerity like that. And when occasionally one hears of a church organisation charging excessive rents from the poor, or a bishop running off with a barmaid, we feel swindled and let down. We say, 'It doesn't matter what a man believes so long as he is sincere.'

But, attractive though it is, it will not do. If you tell me that you believe it, I shall conclude — you must be joking. Here are three good reasons why I can't accept it.

LIFE TEACHES US THAT SINCERITY IS NOT ENOUGH

A moment's reflection will show what a ludicrous creed it is! We would never apply it to matters we consider important, would we? Take politics, for instance. What politician would accept for a moment that it does not matter what you believe so long as you are sincere? That would obliterate the difference between Monarchist and Republican, between Socialist and Capitalist, between Nationalist and Progressive. On that view it would be impossible to censure Russia's invasion of Czechoslovakia. On that view you could whitewash Hitler's ruthless slaughter of six million Jews in pursuit of *Herrenvolk* policy! No, in politics it matters enormously what you believe.

We would never apply this argument about sincerity being enough to economics, say, or to examinations. Who could suppose that it doesn't matter what firm you invest your money in so long as you sincerely believe that it is sound? Who would maintain that it does not matter what you believe when you write an examination? You can put down sense or nonsense; it makes no difference, so long as you are sincere! As we all know to our cost, you can be very sincere and very wrong.

Actually, you'd never get to work in the morning if you operated on this sincerity principle. No matter what earnest beliefs you held about the public transport system, you would miss your train and fail to reach your destination if you took no notice of the timetable but continued to maintain that it does not mattter what a man believes so long as he is sincere.

Pause to reflect on it for a moment. The outlook we have been considering is not merely ridiculous, but cruel. Just think of applying it to advising a crippled man when to cross a busy road: 'It doesn't matter what you believe about the speed and frequency of cars. Just carry on sincerely towards the other side, and you'll be all right!' Liberal and tolerant though it seemed to begin with, this outlook turns out to be cynical and cruel. Under the guise of charity this maxim hides a callous indifference to truth. It is little short of criminal.

Yes, life teaches us unequivocally that it matters enormously what we believe. We need to be sincere: we also need to be right.

THE BIBLE TEACHES US THAT SINCERITY IS NOT ENOUGH

Now, you may or may not be inclined to take the Bible as a final authority about God. But you must at least recognise that it is the most significant book in the world, has done more than any other book to change the world for good, remains the world's best seller, and was composed over a period of some fifteen hundred years. So it may be worth listening to. It may well embody perspective and wisdom, for it comprises a very broad spectrum of human history and experience. What does it have to say on whether sincerity is enough?

Take, first, a man like Abraham, the father of the Jewish nation. If you were to ask him whether sincerity was enough, he would reply 'Far from it. I was sincere when I lived in Ur of the Chaldees. But God called me out. I believed him, and obeyed. God promised to raise up a family and indeed a nation out of my loins, when both I and my wife were too old to have children. I believed him — and here is Isaac my son to show you how much belief matters. Why, the whole latter part of my life has been based on the conviction that what you believe is fundamental to what you do and what you are.' What Abraham became in virtue of his faith in God is graphically summarised in Hebrews 11: 8–19 (if you find the longer account, starting in Genesis 14, too much to cope with).

Noah would never have agreed for a moment that it doesn't matter what you believe so long as you are sincere. No doubt his neighbours were very sincere in thinking they were all right. But Noah's sincerity was of a different stamp. It sprang from his belief that God had called him to build an ark in which those who took refuge would be safe from the waters of the flood. Belief led to action.

Naaman, the great Syrian general, was a stickler for sincerity. He sincerely believed that Elisha the prophet would come out to him 'and stand and call on the name of the Lord his God and strike his hand over the place and heal the leprosy'. He sincerely believed that if washing in a river was to be the prescription, the cool, clear waters of his native Abana and Pharpar would do every bit as much good as Israel's muddy Jordan. He was sincere, but wrong. If he had not admitted as much and changed his attitude, he would never have been healed.

The night of the Exodus, when the escape of the Israelites from Egypt cemented them fully into a nation, was another case in point. You will recall the story. Only those households who sacrificed a lamb and splashed some of its blood above the doorpost of their home were spared the death of their firstborn. Only they left Egypt unharmed. If a father had said, 'Oh, it doesn't matter about that silly old blood on the lintel. Let's get a good night's sleep in preparation for the journey,' he might well have been sincere, but he'd have been wrong, his firstborn son would have been dead, and there would have been no Promised Land for him.

The New Testament attitude is the same. The Pharisees are the outstanding examples of people, highly religious people at that, who thought they were O.K. — and they were not. Pontius Pilate seeems to have been a fairly sincere governor of a difficult province, Judea: he may well have believed it would be in the general interest for Jesus to be liquidated — but he was wrong. Saul of Tarsus believed he could put himself in the right with God by meticulously keeping the Law and zealously persecuting the heretics — but he came to realise that his sincere attempt was a hopeless failure. Saul, the fanatical, self-righteous persecutor, who became Paul, the dedicated, loving apostle, is a splendid example of the fact that sincerity is not enough. It matters what you believe.

JESUS TEACHES US THAT SINCERITY IS NOT ENOUGH

It would be difficult to find anyone more sincere than the rich young ruler: but we read that he went away sorrowful, because he did not believe enough in Jesus to give him priority over his money.

Nobody could have been more sincere than the Pharisees. They were meticulous in their worship, fastidious in keeping clear of any defilement, and dedicated to keeping the Law of God. They were sincere — but wrong. It was these very Pharisees whom Jesus had to describe as a viper's brood: it was they who, he observed, 'would not come to me so as to receive life' (John 5: 40). Sincere in their practice, they were mistaken in their belief, and Jesus was more stringent in his condemnation of those dedicated, sincere men than of the quislings and the prostitutes whom they despised. It does matter what you believe. So much so that when the Jews, anxious to please God by *doing* something, came and asked Jesus 'What shall we do so that we may do what pleases God?', he replied, 'This is what pleases God — to *believe* in him whom he has sent' (John 6: 28f).

SINCERITY AND BELIEF

Nowhere in the Gospels does Jesus stress more powerfully the supreme importance of belief than in the best known verse of the whole Bible. 'God so loved the world that he gave his only Son, that whosoever believes in him should not perish but have eternal life' (John 3: 16). The passage continues, 'The man who believes in him is not condemned: he who does not believe is condemned already, because he has not believed in the name of the only Son of God. And this is the condemnation, that light has come into the world, and men loved darkness rather than light because their deeds were evil.' God, you see, not sincerity, is the supreme reality. And God saw that man was perishing, on the way to final ruin, because it is all too easy to be sincere, and wrong. So God did something about it. He sent Jesus who was one with himself and yet distinct from himself — Son is maybe the best human analogy. Jesus lived and died for the express purpose of rescuing us, and enabling us to enjoy a new quality of life, eternal life.

There is just one condition. We are called to believe! Jesus goes on to make it plain that we will not be ruined by our evil ways, which, to some extent, we cannot help. We will be ruined by failing to trust the one who has brought the remedy for our sick condition. The Light has come into the world. The Bridge back to God has been established. It is up to us to believe or reject: we have the choice, and we shall be held responsible for our decision. 'The man who believes in him is not condemned': no, for Another has borne his condemnation. 'But he who does not believe is condemned already', not because he is a sinner (which he is) but because he has been fool enough to reject the remedy. Do not, I beg you, commit this ultimate folly under the claim of tolerance. If there happens to be only one antitoxin for a disease, it is not charity but folly to say, 'It doesn't matter whether you take it or not, so long as you are sincere.' And we all have the disease. It has affected our past. It dogs our present. It threatens our future.

THE LIMITATIONS OF SINCERITY

Can sincerity alter the past? I think of a gangster who found Christ in prison — and I can see him now, out of prison, reconciled with his wife, accepted and loved in a Christian community. He has been released from his past. Sincerity could never produce a change like that. Only Jesus can. Belief in Jesus puts you in touch with the one who died to clean up your past. 'There is no condemnation to the man who is in Christ Jesus' (Romans 8: 1).

Can sincerity alter a man's life in the present? I think of an obsessive gambler who had tried everything to break the habit, and had failed. He discovered that sincerity is not enough. And then he came to Christ. The Spirit of Jesus came into his life, and at once the old slavery to gambling was broken. Not so surprising after all, is it? You'd expect Jesus to make a difference, and he does. I think of a couple whose marriage was breaking up, though they had sincerely tried to make a go of it. But once they both came to terms with Christ, and welcomed his Spirit into their lives, they found each other afresh and are now living a happy and useful Christian life.

Or think of the future. Can sincerity set our minds at rest about death and what follows death? Anyone who has attended the dying knows that it cannot. But the one who rose from the dead, the one who 'holds the keys of death and the after-life', he can take away the dread of death and hell. I think of an old friend of mine, a bishop in China and for years director of one of the biggest missionary agencies in the world. When his time came to die, he asked for the Hallelulia Chorus from the Messiah to be played, murmured 'Wonderful!' and passed joyfully into his Master's presence. Like Handel, like Christians all down the ages, he pinned his faith for the future not in sincerity or tolerance, but in the Risen One.

Do you now see why belief is so important? The Lord offers us so much; the cross to lift the burden of the past; the Spirit to change the selfishness of our lives; the resurrection to assure us of a future with him. Three firm, objective realities — no mere sincerity. No wonder the reformers in the sixteenth century used to rejoice in three great mottoes:

> *Sola gratia* — by God's free goodness alone
> *Sola fide* — through faith alone
> *Soli Deo gloria* — and to God alone be the glory!

Incidentally, aren't you glad that we are not judged by our sincerity? What a burden that would impose on every minute of the day; on the motivation of every action; on the expression of every word. The word 'sincere' comes from the Latin *sine cera*, 'without wax'. It is a metaphor derived from bee-keeping. Quality honey has to be wax free, and the Greek word for 'sincere', literally 'judged in the light of the sun' shows how you decided the matter. Why, if I were judged in the blazing sunlight of God's holiness, and every word and deed and motive was scrutinised for sincerity, I wouldn't have a hope. Would you? I'm all too aware of insincerity in myself and others to relish a test like that. 'How nice to see you,' we say, when inwardly furious at the interruption. 'I haven't the time', we say, when faced with something we don't want to do. 'What about those who have never heard the gospel?' we ask, when the wonder and challenge of what Christ has done drives us into a corner. Shallow insincerities, all of them! Even the glib claim that sincerity is all we need itself reeks of insincerity. We do not apply it to any other area of life: it is just an excuse, to evade facing up to the light.

When I am confronted by the God who is too holy to tolerate evil in those he loves, the God whose eyes are like flaming fire — then I am thankful that I shall have something more substantial than sincerity to rely on. I shall be resting my weight on the Jesus in whom I have believed. How about you?

Four questions, as I close this chapter.

WHY IS BELIEVING SO IMPORTANT?

For two good reasons. Partly, because belief is the basis for action. It is foolish to concentrate on sincerity of action if you are casual about the nature of your beliefs. What you believe leads inevitably to what you do and what you are.

But there is an even more important answer to this question. Believing is so important because it is the only conceivable response to love. When God's love is brought to me in Christ, I merely insult him if I say, 'Right, that's very nice of you. Now how about a bit of churchgoing, a bit of sincerity and turning over a new leaf so as to earn your love?' The only proper response to such a generous and undeserved gift is to stretch out the hand of faith and say 'Thank you'.

WHAT DOES BELIEVING ACHIEVE?

Once again the answer can be roughly summarised in two parts. First, it clears up the past, or rather, claims the clearing up that Christ achieved on the cross. 'Being acquitted by faith we have peace with God', was St. Paul's triumphant discovery (Romans 5: 1). It's as if I were in prison and all unknown to me a Royal Pardon was being drawn up for me. I would stay in prison along with my accusing record, until I accepted that Royal Pardon, and stepped out of prison, a free man with nothing against my name.

Second, believing brings a man into God's family. 'To as many as received him, or believed on his name, he gave the right to become the children of God', says St. John (John 1: 12). 'We have received the Spirit who adopts us into the family,' says St. Paul (Romans 8: 15). It is as though we were juvenile delinquents, and the judge not only settled our fine himself, but adopted us into his very family alongside his own son. There is nothing we could do to earn it. We would just trustingly accept the new relationship, say 'Thank you', and try to live lives worthy of it.

WHAT WILL BELIEVING INVOLVE?

It is certainly no cheap option, no easy alternative to costly action. But neither does believing mean that we are committed to endless dreary and legalistic observances. Look at it like this. What will believing in his coach mean to the athlete? What will believing in his teacher mean to the pupil? What will believing in his doctor mean for the patient? What will belief in the parent mean for the child, or the husband for the wife? Certainly discipline and obedience will be part of the total package; but somehow it will not be irksome, because of the relationship. That is what it is like to believe in Jesus. It is a lifelong commitment, a dependence on and an ever-growing obedience to the one who has shown himself to be utterly reliable. Because he came to this world in order to seek me; because he died for me and rose for me; because he offers to share my very life and enter the inmost recesses of my being, I know I can trust him to the full. And what is belief if not trust?

HOW DO I ACTUALLY BELIEVE?

Once again, there are two parts to it. Having got past the stage of thinking that faith is believing what you know is not true, or that it consists in reciting the creeds parrot fashion, it resolves itself into a matter for the head and a matter for the will.

Let's look at the intellectual side first. Belief is no surrender of the intellect. It is no blind acceptance of everything in the Bible, or every dogma of the Christian church. No. Belief is concerned with Jesus Christ. If you like, Jesus is God's right hand of fellowship stretched out to us. Belief is our hand of response, stretched out to him. The two need to meet. I ask you, then, do you believe that Jesus Christ is the Son of God? Do you believe he died for you? Do you believe he is the risen Lord, willing and able to change your life? That is the hard core of Christian belief. The early Christians summarised it in the famous fish symbol — for the five letters which go to make up the Greek word for fish could be seen as the first letters of the following claims about Jesus: 'Jesus Christ, Son of God, Saviour'. Those claims take you to the nerve centre of Christian belief.

But it is all too easy to believe things in your head without getting personally involved with them, or acting on them. That is why it is vital to realise that belief is a matter not only of the mind but of the will. This delightful story about Blondin, the celebrated tightrope-walker of a hundred years ago, makes the point with humour and clarity. He specialised in crossing the Niagara Falls on a tightrope. Variations included crossing blindfold, swathed in a sack, at night, on stilts, and with his feet tied up in blankets. In 1860 he performed before the then Prince of Wales who was visiting Niagara as part of a tour. Blondin offered to carry him over on his back. The Prince declined, but with royal graciousness suggested that the Duke of Newcastle, who was in attendance, might like to accept. Unfortunately the Duke of Newcastle, too, refused!

Now those two men believed, in the intellectual sense, that Blondin could do it, but this was not faith in the full-blooded New Testament sense of the word. There was no act of will, no personal commitment. By way of contrast, Blondin's mother watched him wheel a sack of potatoes over the Falls, and then, at his suggestion, climbed into the wheelbarrow herself and entrusted herself to his skill and balance. She was not disappointed. That is a good example of authentic faith.

How about you and Jesus Christ? Do you believe in him with your head? Then put yourself at his disposal. Climb into the wheelbarrow, so to speak, and tell him that you realise sincerity is not enough, that you entrust your life to him, and that you don't mind who knows it.

A genuine act of self-surrender like that will give birth to a growing conviction that Christ, not merely sincerity, is what you need in this life and the next. For the act of commitment leads on to a life of companionship with him who makes all things new — even for you.

7

'I do my best. No man can do more'

CHRISTIANITY is a rescue religion. That is why it is so unpopular. It goes to the heart of human nature and makes a radical difference. But when men pause from the rat race for a moment to take a long cool look at themselves in the light of their own standards, they tend to come up with two main attitudes. One takes a rosy view of human nature, and says in effect, 'I do my best. That ought to be good enough for whatever God there may be. I'll be O.K.' The other is much more pessimistic and says, 'I've made a mess of things. Nothing can alter the past.' We'll look at them in turn: the optimist in this chapter, and the pessimist in the next. They are closely connected, in actual fact. They are two opposite reactions to the problem of guilt.

THE PROBLEM OF GUILT

However hard boiled you are, there are times when you feel dirty, rotten, guilty. It may nag away at you for years, as it did in one of the Great Train Robbers, Buster Edwards, who found he could not live with it and eventually gave himself up. It may just hit you once in a while, as it comes through in Roger McGough's poem, *Come Close and Sleep Now*.

> It is afterwards
> and you talk on tiptoe
> happy to be part
> of the darkness,
> lips becoming limp,
> a prelude to tiredness.
> Come close and sleep now,
> for in the morning
> when a policeman
> disguised as the sun
> creeps into the room:
> and your mother
> disguised as the birds
> calls from the trees,
> you will put on a dress of guilt
> and shoes with broken high ideals
> and refusing coffee
> run all the way home.

That puts it very clearly and movingly. 'Shoes with broken high ideals'. We all wear them. What are we to do about it?

Well, the obvious thing is to forget about it. Just too bad it happened, but no point in making yourself miserable over spilt milk. Forget it. Ah, but that is not so easy. Something over half of the hospital beds in Britain are taken up with people suffering from some form of anxiety. Over 3,000 million pills are issued annually by our doctors in order to counter depression and anxiety. People have pushed unwelcome aspects of their characters down into the subconscious, and those aspects have refused to go away; they continue to trouble us. I have been engaged recently in some group counselling in which primal repressions of terrifying power have been brought back from that area of the subconscious, and once they were dealt with, dramatic bodily healings have taken place. We human beings are complicated creatures, and to repress our sense of guilt about the past solves nothing: it merely builds up trouble for the future.

And even if it didn't, we should still be in queer street. Suppose a man commits murder, and doesn't get caught; suppose he tries to forget about it, and determines to never do such a thing again — what would happen if the evidence should come to light thirty years later, as it has with some of the Nazi war criminals? The answer is simple: the man is guilty however much he has tried to forget it, however long ago he did it, however hard he has tried to go straight in the meantime. Forgetting it does no good, even in the realm of human justice.

Then what is God to do about human failures? Is he to say, 'Well, let's forget it'? Not the God I read of in the Bible! In a way, I wish he would: it would make it so much easier for me, and, I suspect, for you. But on second thoughts I am glad God is not like that — soft, spineless, devoid of justice, pretending that black is white and white is black when we all know perfectly well that such is not the case. Yes, I'm glad God is holy and opposed to human wickedness. Heaven would be hell otherwise.

Not that it matters very much what I hope God may be like. I couldn't possibly know, unless he has revealed himself. And that he has done. He did it in personal terms, in Jesus Christ — no less, as we saw in chapter 5. And Jesus taught more severely about the judgment of God than any of the Old Testament prophets ever did. Remember, it was Jesus who taught about the two ways a man could go: one led to God and the other to destruction. There were two groups a man could belong to: wheat, destined for the barn, or weeds, destined for the fire. There were two destinies that awaited men: inside the joyous feast, or outside where there was weeping and gnashing of teeth. The teaching of Jesus flies straight in the face of our easy-going optimism that God is a good fellow and won't be too fussy about our achievements. He is good, and therefore he will be extremely fussy. He is the ethically upright God that our conscience uncomfortably suggests he is. He is deeply concerned at the fundamental difference between right and wrong, and will not pretend that the distinction is unreal. He will by no means clear the guilty. The Almighty does not owe us forgiveness, any more than the world owes us a living. Forgiveness is never cheap.

WORKING OUR PASSAGE

All down the ages men have had an inkling of this fact. Forgiveness is never cheap: it is costly, and therefore they must do something to pay for it, to earn it. In a very real sense all religions have their root and their unity in this fact. Man must do something, must achieve something, in order to atone for his failures, to make the Almighty gracious to him. All over the world, all down the ages, man has been trying to earn his passage to heaven. He has been saying, in effect, 'I'm a good fellow. I do my best. Surely that is enough?' It may be through mechanical ways like the Tibetan prayer wheel, animistic ways like worship of the spirits of the ancestors, Communist ways like adoration at the tomb of Lenin, Islamic ways like making the pilgrimage to Mecca. It may be through Eastern ways like the Eightfold Path, or mortification of the body in order to gain a better reincarnation. It may be through Western ways like trying harder, seeking to be decent, never doing anyone any harm, doing our best (and who can do more than that?).

This attempt to establish ourselves is exceptionally common in church circles. 'I've been baptised, and confirmed and married in church — and I'm having the kids sent to Sunday school. I go myself at Christmas — I mean, Christmas wouldn't be the same without going to church and singing those carols, would it?' In ways like this we pay our tiny premium for what we hope, when we stop to think about it, will be a whacking great heavenly insurance policy.

But despite its popularity, despite its prevalence all over the world, in every religious system and the irreligious ones as well, this road is a dead end. It is utterly misguided. And I will show you why.

IT IS SHALLOW

It allows us to rely on deeds, not attitude. It is depressingly superficial and external. Would it satisfy any loving parent if his offspring kept the bedroom tidy and cleaned his shoes but never gave him a kiss, never spent time with him? Of course not. But are we to suppose that the Heavenly Father will be overjoyed to welcome us when we haven't said so much as 'Hello' to him from one year's end to another, but smugly claim, 'I've done lots of good things. I do my best. No man can do more.'?

Listen to Jesus' analysis of the human condition. There is nothing external, superficial or shallow about it. He says that 'from within, out of the heart of man, come evil thoughts, acts of ruthless greed, murder, theft, pride and folly' (Mark 7: 21, 22). Of course we know how to do good things. But that does not change the fundamental twist in our natures: 'you, being evil, know how to give good gifts to your children . . .' (Luke 11: 13) observed the master Physician. You cannot get rid of a cancerous growth by using lots of make-up and running round helping everyone else in the house. It needs drastic surgery. Doing good deeds may well merely drive the dirt under the carpet. It is a very shallow remedy for the human situation. 'It is essential not to have faith in human nature,' wrote Professor

Butterfield, the famous historian: 'Such a belief is very recent and very disastrous.' To reject the doctrine of human wickedness means that you will always be perplexed when you hear the perversity of man on the news each evening; you will always be puzzled by the prevalence of racism, by the exploitation of the helpless, by the oppression of the weak by the strong, and by the quirks in your own behaviour. One celebrated atheist, turned Christian, put it like this. 'To reject the doctrine of human sinfulness, as so many left-wing rationalists do, was to fall victim to the shallow optimism which led men to believe that the millennium was just round the corner, waiting to be introduced by a society of adequately psychoanalysed, prosperous Socialists. It is because we rejected the doctrine of sin that we on the Left were always being disappointed.' So wrote Professor C. E. M. Joad after a lifetime of persuading himself that he was a good chap at heart, and that provided he did his best he'd be all right.

The truth is that our deeds cannot make up for ourselves. That is why Jesus hammered those good-living, religious Pharisees. It is all too possible to have a façade of goodness and religious observance, but all the time to ignore the disease beneath. Jesus Christ demands a more radical solution.

IT IS IMPOSSIBLE

You and I can't get to heaven on our own good deeds, for the simple reason that they are not good enough for God.

'What?' you say. 'I'm a good-living chap. I've kept the Ten Commandments.' Have you? I wonder. Have you kept the first commandment of all, to give God number one place in your life? I haven't. Jesus said it meant loving the Lord our God with all our heart and mind and soul and strength. I simply haven't begun to keep that first and greatest commandment. I break it every day. And that is not a very encouraging start as I set out to establish myself before God as the fine fellow who does his best and can't be expected to do more.

I glanced down the other commandments. I must not make

my own image of God? Well, I don't make graven images, of course. But I do tend to say 'I can't believe in a God who . . .' or 'The God I believe in is like this . . .' I make him in my image, rather than stopping to find out what he has revealed himself to be in the Bible.

I must not take the name of God in vain? I do it every day without thinking. Keeping the Sabbath day holy, one day in seven separate for God and family and rest? Don't make me laugh. Honour father and mother? Not likely. When I'm young I rebel against them as hard as I can. When I'm married I neglect them. When they are old I stuff them in an old people's home. Honour them indeed!

I feel a bit better seeing the command not to kill. I have never done that. But hang on a minute: didn't Jesus say something about the man who hates being just as repulsive to God as the man who gives vent to his hatred in murder?

It's the same with that command about adultery. I may not have gone in for the wife-swapping parties that some of my friends indulge in. But how about that dance when I went a lot further than I intended? How about the lustful thoughts that jostle through my mind whenever I see a shapely woman? Yes, Jesus was right when he put those thoughts down to just the same weakness in human nature as produces adultery.

'Thou shalt not steal.' But I'm afraid I do. Steal goods from the shops, when nobody is looking; steal a free ride from the bus, when the conductor doesn't notice; steal from the tax man by getting paid in cash not by cheque; yes, it happens. And as for not bearing false witness against my neighbour, why, that's what sells the Sunday papers. A little bit of scandal, a bit of exaggeration, of character assassination, of making myself look big in comparison with him. That final command against coveting, against unrestrained desire for what is not mine — man, the whole of our society is built on covet-ousness! You covet the next man's car and his wife and his washing machine and his freezer and his colour T.V. and . . . Don't be stupid; life is built on coveting. O.K. then, but don't turn round and tell me that you have kept the Ten Com-

mandments and are therefore a splendid chap whom God ought
to be proud to know. You have broken the lot. And so have I.

'Well, at any rate I live by the Sermon on the Mount.' It is
amazing how many people think they do. I always feel they
must be joking. The standards of the Sermon on the Mount
make the Ten Commandments look like kid's stuff. Do you
hunger and thirst after what is right? Are you among the pure
in heart who will see God? Are you a peacemaker at home and
in industry? Do you allow yourself to be wronged, persecuted
even, for the sake of what is right? Do you go and get reconciled with the chap whose guts you hate before presenting
yourself in church with your offering? Are you perfect in undis-
criminating concern for the good of all you meet, as your
Heavenly Father is, who makes his rain to fall equally on the
just and the unjust? 'Don't be anxious about tomorrow: trust
your Father, who looks after flowers and birds,' says the
Sermon. Do you live like that?'Don't say,"what shall we eat, or
drink, or wear?" But seek first God's kingly rule and his
righteousness, and all these things will be added to you,' says
the Sermon. Do you live like that? No, of course you don't, and
neither do I. Then we ought to be very careful of boasting that
we live by the Sermon on the Mount. For that Sermon con-
cludes with the solemn assurance that if we do not follow the
teaching of Jesus in this Sermon we face ruin. 'Every man who
hears these words of mine and does them,' says Jesus, 'shall be
like a wise man who built his house upon the rock. And the rain
fell and the floods came and the winds blew and beat upon that
house, but it did not fall because it was founded upon the rock.
And every one who hears these words of mine and does not do
them will be like a foolish man who built his house upon the
sand. And the rain fell and the floods came and the winds blew
and beat against that house, and it fell. And great was the fall
of it' (Matthew 7: 24ff).

On that day it will not do to say, 'Lord, I did my best and
even went to church from time to time.' The Sermon tells us he
will reply, 'Not every one who says to me "Lord, Lord" shall
enter the Kingdom of Heaven, but he who does the will of my

Father who is in heaven. On that day many will say to me "Lord, Lord, did we not prophesy in your name, and cast out demons in your name, and do many mighty works in your name?" And then I will declare to them, "I never knew you. Depart from me, you evildoers" ' (Matthew 7: 21ff).

There sounds the death knell for all man's attempts to justify himself before God. It cannot be done. 'Whoever shall keep the whole law and yet offend in one point, is guilty of all,' says the Epistle of James (2: 10), perceptively. After all, if I am had up for speeding, it won't help me to say that I have never robbed a bank and never mugged an old woman. I am guilty of speeding. I am in trouble. With God I have broken his law daily, hourly. I am in deep trouble. And it will be a very thin excuse to say 'I've done my best.' For one thing, to be honest, I haven't. And for another, my best is not good enough for a holy God. I need something a lot better than my best if I'm going to get right with him. I find that the Bible is very unflattering about my attempts to doll myself up in the sight of God. It tells me that all my righteousnesses (my righteousnesses, mark you!) are like filthy rags, let alone the things I know are not much good. It implies that I have been looking in one of those distorting mirrors and hold too high a view of my own achievements and too low a view of God's nature and demands. 'The heart is deceitful above all things and desperately corrupt; who can understand it? I, the Lord, search the mind and try the heart, and give to every man according to his ways, according to the fruit of his doings' (Jeremiah 17: 9). No, if that is the standard, if those are the stakes, then I can't compete. I begin to see that it is impossible that my best should be good enough for God.

IT IS INTOLERABLE

If heaven were the reward of merit, it would be ghastly. If I got there because I did my best, pushed my way in, and established my own claims no matter who got hurt in the process, it would be intolerable. If heaven were peopled by self-made men waving their own beastly goodness around under every one else's nose, it would be hell. Ascot is bad enough, with everyone showing off their clothes for all they are worth. Is heaven to be one long Ascot? Perish the thought!

I found a gravestone once, in an ancient church. It enshrined superbly this idea that I do my best and God ought to be very pleased with it, and it shows how repulsive that idea really is. It comes from King Ethelred the Unready, and it runs like this:

I, Ethelred, king of Albion, in order that on the awful day of judgment I may, by the intercession of the saints, be deemed worthy to be admitted to the heavenly kingdom, do give Almighty God the possession of three lands [i.e. farms] to be held for ever for the monastery of the aforesaid martyr.

That shows up the proud attitude of 'I do my best. What man can do more?' in its true colours. It is disgusting. God will not have his heaven cluttered up with the smug and the self-satisfied. The very idea is obscene.

Paul put it like this. Writing to some very self-satisfied Galatians he said, in effect, 'If you rely on trying your best in order to get to God, you have had it. You fall under the curse which the Law of God imposes on all who break it. Does not the Old Testament say, "Cursed be every one who does not abide by *all* things written in the book of the law, and do them"? You cannot claim obedience like that, can you? Very well, you fall under the judgment of God.' In other words, it is impossible to get through to God on the basis of my own good works. But Paul does not leave it there. He goes on in the very next verse to show that even if it were possible, it would be intolerable. It would mean that a man could put a pistol at God's head, so to speak, and say, 'I've done all these good things. You must make room for me in your heaven even though I have never given you a thought and don't love you the least bit.' So Paul maintains, 'It is quite obvious that nobody gets in touch with God just by doing good things. That would leave the whole principle of trust out of account. And the Old Testament makes it quite clear that it is the man who is made right with God by trusting him, who enjoys life with him for ever. But doing your best has nothing to do with this attitude of trust: it is simply a matter of cold achievement.' That is a rough paraphrase of Galatians 3: 10–12. And it seems to me to be unanswerable. If I rely on doing my best to put me in the clear with God, I shall find not only that it is impossible, because I fail again and again and again; but that the whole idea is intolerable because it leaves me untouched in my pride and self-esteem and takes no account of the loving trust I should have with my heavenly Father.

In a word, all attempts to establish myself before God are bound to fail. He is holy and I am not. My good deeds cannot make up for my crooked heart and my rebellious attitude towards the God I have wronged and from whose gaze I am only too anxious to escape. It is hard and humiliating to have to admit this. That is why so many people prefer to shelter under the bogus refuge of 'I do my best. No man can do more.' But unless I have a better shelter than that, it will let the wind and the rain and the hail in at the Day of Judgment. I need to come to the position of one rich, able, intelligent young pleasure-seeker, sixteen centuries ago, who was man enough to face up to the unpalatable truth and get right with God on God's terms, not his own. He wrote, 'You took me, God, from behind my own back where I had put myself all the time I preferred not to see myself. And you set me before my face, that I might see how vile I was. I saw myself, and was horrified.' That was Augustine, who later became the famous Christian leader. I fancy we all need to tread that humbling path, if God is to be able to do anything with us. He has no room for big-heads in his family. There is one condition for entry; one only. It is to change our attitude, to come down from our high horse, and be willing to trust him and his way of pardon. What that is we shall see in the next chapter.

8

'Nothing can alter the past'

THIS CHAPTER IS a companion piece to the previous one. Both of them deal with the reactions of human beings to guilt. In the last chapter we were looking at the man who hoped the past would go away, so long as he did his best. In this chapter we are concerned with the person who knows all too well that the past will not go away. It is permanent. Nothing can change it. Its stain us indelible. Often one hears a person bewail some awful incident in their past, and say, 'I can never forgive myself.'

Like Lady Macbeth after the murder, they continue, as it were, for ever going through the motions of washing their hands, but are all too well aware that all the perfumes of Arabia cannot remove the smell of blood from it. Nothing can undo the past.

Their problem, then, is precisely the opposite of the one we looked at in the previous chapter. There the self-made man was confident that he would be all right: he did his best, and what more could be required of him? Here, nothing avails to put the past right. But paradoxical as it may seem, both diseases have the same remedy. It is to be found on a green hill far away, outside a city wall.

THAT MAN ON HIS CROSS

Come with me in imagination to that famous scene. It is a bank holiday. A rough, laughing crowd jostles through the narrow streets of Jerusalem. At last the Roman governor has ratified the decision of the Jewish Council, and given sentence against Jesus of Nazareth. He is to die in the approved fashion for criminals of the lower classes in occupied countries, by crucifixion. The knot of soldiers in charge of the execution push through the crowd. Of the three men they are guarding carefully, one stumbles. He has been kept awake all night, without food or drink, and has had a succession of trials. He is exhausted. He collapses under the weight of the heavy cross beam of his cross which he has to carry. The lack of sleep, food and the loss of blood from his back, lacerated as it was with the Roman cat-o'-nine-tails, prove too much for him. He stumbles to his knees, and the soldiers grab a black man who happens to be passing by. 'You'll do: carry his cross, and look sharp about it.' Soon the execution party comes to a spot outside the city wall, while the crowd watches the spectacle of three public deaths with mingled emotions. The soldiers dig pits for the crosses to go into. The crosses are laid on the ground, and the three men are made to lie on them. Long iron spikes are then nailed through their ankles and their wrists. A few years ago the bones of a crucified man were unearthed in Israel. None had ever been discovered before. The spikes had pierced through the two bones at the wrist and had gone through the ankle. Think of the agony it must have been. No doubt the two criminals executed with Jesus cursed and swore and struggled. Jesus breathed a prayer instead: 'Father, forgive them. They do not know what they are doing.'

The grisly job is done at length. The soldiers lift the crosses one by one and slot them into the ground. The men are now exposed to the gaze of the crowd, suspended between earth and sky, with every nerve in agony, fighting for breath. No quick death awaits them, as they hang in terrible anguish, parched by the heat, distraught by the flies.

A GOD-FORSAKEN PLACE

What accounts for the fascination that central figure on the cross has exercised over nineteen centuries of men? It could not be merely his physical suffering, ghastly as that was. Other men have died in as great pain, perhaps greater. The two brigands executed with him had just as terrible an end. No, his physical sufferings do not get us to the heart of what was achieved on that cross. Interestingly enough, the Gospel writers hardly pause on them at all. 'There they crucified him,' is all they say, sparing us the harrowing detail. Nor can his mental suffering exhaust the mystery. How galling to have priests mocking him: 'He saved others, himself he cannot save. Let Christ the King of Israel come down now from the cross, so that we may see and believe.' How heartbreaking to find all his disciples running for cover. How humiliating to be exposed as a failure, his life's work in ruins. How crushing to be rejected and crucified by God's own people whom he had come to teach and to rescue. His mental sufferings must have broken his heart: but they do not penetrate the mystery of that cross.

Darkness falls, a premature darkness, a darkness which could be felt. Curiously enough a pagan historian, Thallus, records it, so it is no mere colourful exaggeration from the Gospels. But none the less it is highly symbolic of the darkness which engulfed Jesus at that supreme moment of his life. Darkness pierced with his cry of agony, culled from Psalm 22, 'My God, my God, why have you forsaken me?' Darkness matched only by that in the Garden of Gethsemane the night before, when he had faced up to his death and what it would entail, and had sweated blood at the prospect. Why indeed was this best of men allowed to feel bereft, God-forsaken in this his finest hour?

The answer which all different strands of the New Testament give is this. He *felt* cut off from his Heavenly Father for the simple reason that he *was* cut off. Paul, as we saw in the last chapter, was clear that no man could approach God dressed in the clothes of his own good deeds. Because all have broken the law of God, all rest under its curse, its judgment. But if you were to ask Paul what lay at the heart of the cross of Jesus, he would tell you, 'Christ rescued us from the curse of the broken law, *becoming a curse for us.*' Unthinkable — that the holy one, the perfect man, the innocent Son of God should end up in the place of judgment, of cursing. But so it was. As a Jew Paul would have known his Old Testament. He knew very well that passage in Deuteronomy which said that anyone exposed on a cross must be seen as resting under the curse of God. He had felt, in his pre-Christian days, that here was an excellent reason why Jesus could not possibly be the longed-for Messiah of his people; he had ended up not merely in the place of failure, but of cursing. On the road to Damascus he had met the risen Lord Jesus. He had had his previous view shattered. He came to see that Jesus had indeed come to meet his death in the place of cursing, but *the curse was ours* which he gladly bore for us. No wonder he gives up his life in glad service for 'the Son of God who loved me and gave himself for me'. As he reflects on the fantastic exchange of positions which Jesus undertook for us, he can do no other. 'For our sake, God made Jesus who knew no sin *to be sin* for us, Jesus who knew no sin, so that we might become the very goodness of God in him' (2 Corinthians 5: 21). No wonder Jesus felt cut off from God: he was cut off . . . and it was in order to enable us to come near.

WHAT DOES IT MEAN?

The New Testament writers struggle to express this un-dreamed of good news in a variety of metaphors. Fantastic that God should underwrite our debts, and lift our burdens and endure our curse, and carry our guilt. Fantastic, indeed; but it takes us to the very heart of Calvary. That is why Jesus steadfastly set his face to go to Jerusalem — when he might so easily have left for somewhere else. He had an appointment with death. He knew that he was going to endure the destiny of the Suffering Servant, sketched out so graphically in the Old Testament prophecies. He knew that the Lord was going to lay on him the iniquities of us all. He knew that he was going to bear our offences. He knew that the lashes which meant our peace would lacerate him. He knew that his death would be a sacrifice for sin such as no sacrificial system in the world could match — the Lord, offering his life for sinners. He knew that the Son of Man, as he called himself, would give his life as ransom for many, on that cross. He knew that he would see the fruit of his labours after it was all over and be satisfied — feel it was worth it. For he was about to forge a new agreement be-tween God and man, a new covenant. All other covenants in the history of religions had two sides to them, man's side and God's side. That was just the trouble about them — man kept break-ing his side of the bargain! But this covenant would bring for-giveness of sins. It would undertake not only God's side but man's side. On that cross he would be perfect man, offering up his life for others: he would also be perfect God, for 'God was in Christ, reconciling the world to himself, not reckoning their sins up against them.' Such was the divine plan, hidden from all eternity in the purposes of God, but revealed in its horror and its glory on the first Good Friday.

Perhaps we could do worse than look at it from the per-spective of three people present that day. It will give us three pictures, three metaphors of what Jesus achieved for us on that cross; three ways of enabling us to see that even if we can't forgive ourselves for some terrible thing we have done in the past, God can and will forgive, and do so with perfect justice and with boundless love.

THE FREEDOM FIGHTER'S VIEW

There was one man on that first Good Friday who vividly came to understand what the cross of Jesus meant. He was a freedom fighter, caught in the act of armed insurrection and murder. Imprisoned with his mates, he awaited the day of execution, glad that he had knocked off a few Romans, sad that he had not managed to deliver his country from the clutches of Rome. Imagine him waiting as the last morning of his life dawned. The steps along the corridor. The key in the lock. And the hairs on his neck stood up. Then to his amazement, the centurion knocked the chains off his hands and feet and said, 'You're a free man, Barabbas.' Incredulously, Barabbas looked at him, and concluded it was a sick joke. But it was no joke. He heard of Pilate's strange offer to release to the people at that Feast of Passover either himself or another revolutionary leader of a very different kind, another 'Barabbas', which means 'son of the Father'. Dazed, he would have hardly been able to drag himself away from the place of execution where his friends were dying for the crimes they had committed on behalf of their country, and where this strange Son of the Father was dying on Barabbas' very own cross, in Barabbas' very own place. History does not relate what became of him. But he could scarcely have missed the point that Jesus was taking his place. Jesus' death was settling his account so that his crimes would never be brought up against him again. He could scarcely have avoided reflecting that he should by rights have been on that central cross. 'He did it for me,' I can imagine him saying: 'He did it for me.'

That strange exchange made its impression on the Christian community. St. Peter was almost certainly an eyewitness of that scene, skulking at the edge of the crowd where he would not attract unwanted attention. He tells us in his First Letter that he was a 'witness of the sufferings of Christ'. After seeing

Jesus carrying that cross up to the place of execution, stumbling under its weight, nailed to its unwelcome embrace, he wrote to his Christian readers words which are surely to be interpreted in the light of what he saw and felt that day. 'Christ suffered for you,' he writes. 'When he was reviled he did not revile in return; when he suffered, he did not threaten; but he trusted to him who judges justly. He himself bore our sins in his own body up to the tree ... By his wounds you have been healed' (1 Peter 2: 21). Images of the Suffering Servant of Isaiah, of Jesus staggering up to Golgotha bearing the load of Peter's sins, of the innocent Jesus in the place of us guilty Barabbases, may all have struggled through his mind as he wrote. He put it with great clarity in the next chapter (1 Peter 3: 18). 'For Christ also suffered for sins, once for all, the righteous for the unrighteous, that he might bring us to God.' That was why he died: the righteous in the place of the unrighteous. Peter had understood what the cross was all about.

So had Paul. In a remarkable passage in his letter to the Colossians, he tells us that God has forgiven us all our sins, having cancelled the list of failures which stood against our names, with its legal demands: he swept it aside, nailing it to his cross. What a sublime understanding of Calvary! There was a long list of crimes against Barabbas, but Jesus met them all when he died in Barabbas' place on that central cross. There was a long list of much more refined sins against Paul's name; but Jesus met them all when he died in Paul's place, on that central cross. The condemned criminal usually had a charge sheet with his crime written on it hung round his neck as he went out to execution; this was nailed on to his cross. And Paul sees Jesus going out to die with — not his jeering accusation 'King of the Jews' round his neck, but with Paul's sins, your sins and my sins, hung round his neck. That is why he died. To square our account. To clear our debt to the God we have wronged. He swept aside all the accusing failures which I have written against myself through my wilful sins: and he nailed them to Christ's cross. They will never be raised again with me, any more than they will with Paul, with Peter, with Barabbas.

For Christ has once suffered for sins, the righteous for the unrighteous, that he might bring us to God. That is one aspect of the meaning of the cross. It settles our debts. It sweeps them aside. It means they will never be raised against us again. For God in Christ has paid the account to the uttermost farthing; even though it took him to that bitter cross in order to do so. Nothing we can do can alter our guilty past. But this act of supreme generosity on his past has altered everything.

THE EXECUTIONER'S VIEW

There was another most interesting character at that cross. We do not know his name, but he made his own impression on the Christian community, for the story is told in no less than three of the Gospels. He was the centurion in charge of the execution squad. He had the closest view of anyone on that grim occasion. He watched Jesus suffer with dignity. He noticed that Jesus was concerned entirely for others, the soldiers who had nailed him there, the mother who had borne him, and the criminals executed with him. He had heard the priests mocking Jesus; he had seen the crowd jeering. He had felt the uncanny darkness: he had heard the great cry as Jesus died. And he burst out with a confession of faith in this man he had just executed. 'Truly this man was the Son of God,' is the bit Matthew and Mark record. Luke's account is more politically slanted: 'Certainly this man was innocent.' Maybe he said both, convinced not only of the innocence of Jesus but of his superhuman quality. Quite what a Roman centurion would have meant by 'Son of God' we cannot be sure. It was one of the titles by which the Emperor liked to be known: so on any showing it was a fantastic confession of loyalty to a crucified member of a subject race. But we can hardly doubt that the evangelists meant us to see far more in that cry. It was the primitive Christian creedal confession: Jesus Christ is Son of God and Saviour. Here was the man who killed Jesus recognising in him the way back to God!

I think we can be pretty sure that this interpretation is correct. In the verses immediately preceding, the evangelists do a curious but deliberate thing. First, they record the death of Jesus: 'Jesus breathed his last.' They then seem to ruin this climax in their story by a ludicrous bit of irrelevant information: 'And the curtain of the temple was ripped in half from the top to the bottom.' They then come back to Calvary and tell us of the centurion's confession of faith. What are they trying to convey?

It is not difficult to discover, once we recall what the curtain in the temple was for. It was intended to guard the holiest part of the temple from intruders. Nobody was to go into that 'Holy of Holies' except the high priest, once a year, on the Day of Atonement. He then made sacrifice for his own sins and for the sins of the people by shedding the blood of an animal and offering it on the altar. The curtain meant exclusion: it meant that God was holy, and man was not. It was a vast visual aid to get one simple message across, that God is too holy for sinful folk like you and me to approach. It spelt 'Keep out'.

When Jesus died on that cross the temple curtain was split: it was an act of God, and was probably due to an earthquake that the Jewish historian Josephus says took place about that time and shook the lintels of the temple. But however it happened, its message was loud and clear to those Christian evangelists. It spelt 'Come in'. It meant that Jesus, the supreme high priest, had made the ultimate sacrifice not for his own sins (he had none to atone for) but for those of a whole world gone astray. It meant that those who trusted him could now draw near to God without fear that they would be excluded. And listen to the way that confident access resounds through the New Testament. 'Now through Jesus Christ you who once were afar off have been brought near in the blood of Christ,' says the Letter to the Ephesians (2: 13), and 'Through him we both [Jews and Gentiles alike] have access in one Spirit to the Father' (2: 18). In his letter to the Romans Paul thrills to the wonder of our acquittal through what Jesus did on that cross. 'We have peace with God through our Lord Jesus Christ,' he cries: 'through him we have obtained access' (5: 1). And the writer to the

Hebrews puts it a bit more allegorically but very powerfully, when he writes: 'Brothers, we have confidence to enter the Holy of Holies through the blood of Jesus, the new and living way which has opened for us through the curtain, that is his flesh . . .' (10: 19). His flesh offered for us on that cross made the way into God's holy presence possible; it split the curtain, so to speak, which kept God so distant and unreal. And instead of one man going in once a year after due sacrifice — repeated annually — we can all go in at any time. There is unrestricted access into the holy presence of God for all who trust the one whose death made it all possible. That death meant access. And we find the centurion making no delay to take that access — achieved through the death of Jesus for which he had been responsible. We are meant to see ourselves in that centurion, just as we are in Barabbas. The death of Jesus settles our account, and means we can go straight into the presence of God unafraid, knowing that the barriers have been broken down, the guilt has been expiated, the dirt washed away by the death of Jesus, the Saviour. And that is good news for troubled consciences which no psychiatry can match.

THE DYING ROBBER'S VIEW

The third figure at the cross of Jesus who catches our attention is the robber who hangs beside him. As they suffer there together, this man makes the most remarkable statement in the whole astounding narrative. He says, 'Jesus, remember me when you come in your kingly power.' The other criminal executed alongside them had been cursing at the silent sufferer. 'Messiah, are you? O.K. then, save yourself — and us!' But the man we have come to know as the penitent thief rebuked him. 'Do you not fear God? You are going to meet him soon enough! And neither you nor I can complain: we are getting what we deserve. But this man has done nothing wrong.' It was then that he turned to Jesus with his fascinating request, 'Jesus, remember me when you come in your kingly power.' What a fantastic example of faith that was. To believe that the man executed alongside you had a future, and would be able to remember you. To believe that he had a kingdom and would come in his kingly rule. To turn to a bloodied, suffering man in his death throes and ask for favourable memory in the life to come — I find it simply staggering. But that is what he did. And Jesus replied with one of the greatest of all his sayings: 'Today you will be with me in Paradise.' Marvellous to know that he would die today — often men lingered on for a day or two after crucifixion. Marvellous to know that he would be with Jesus. Marvellous to have that future described in a lovely old Persian word for a park or garden, the garden of God. But most marvellous of all is the implication which, though unspoken, comes through like a trumpet blast. This man's accusing past will be silenced: his guilt will be expiated; his sins will be forgotten. He will be with Jesus in God's garden. He had done nothing to deserve it: how could he do a thing to earn his forgiveness when he was hanging there on a cross, dying? Not a thing could he contribute to his own salvation — except the sin from which he needed to be saved. But that, St. Luke would seem to teach us, is precisely the condition of being forgiven. 'Nothing in my hand I bring: simply to thy cross I cling.' It is not the churchmen with lots of religious observances to their name; it is not the Romans with all their political power and influence; but a simple, guilty, condemned criminal who finds pardon with Jesus.

Do ... or done?

That is why the New Testament writers make such a point of telling us that we are not put right with God by anything that we do; rather by something done for us. The worldly man's religion has two letters in it: 'do'. The forgiven sinner's has four: 'done'. And in that 'done' countless people of every age and culture have found peace. 'There is no condemnation to the man who is in Christ Jesus,' writes Paul. 'For what our attempts to keep the law could never do God himself has done through the person and the death of Jesus.' Done! It reminds me of the little girl who was so thrilled when she came to understand the meaning of the cross. 'I'm trusting in the justice of God, Mummy,' she cried. 'You mean in the love of God, dear?' corrected her mother. 'Oh no,' said the little girl. 'Jesus has died and paid all my debts. And God won't charge me for them again. I'm trusting in the justice of God.' How right she was.

I met this summer a remarkable man, quiet, confident. He had been a dance-band leader. And on his way home in the car one night he had been listening to a snatch of a religious radio programme. The preacher asked, 'If you were to die tonight, what possible reason is there why God should allow you into his heaven?' That seemed to James Kennedy a good question. So he did not rest until he discovered the answer. He knew that if his acceptance depended on his own good deeds he would have every reason to feel despondent. But he came to see that it didn't depend on anything of the sort. His acceptance, his pardon, his future with God depended simply and solely on what God had done to make him acceptable: it rested on the cross of Jesus Christ. That discovery revolutionised his life. He trained for ordination and is now exercising a remarkable ministry in the U.S.A. in which this question, that changed his life, features largely. Hundreds if not thousands of people each year come to God through the outreach of that church, as its members go round visiting and asking folk, 'If you died tonight, what good reason is there why God should accept you into his heaven?'

What would you say to that question? If you are just a churchman, if you are an 'I do my best' type, you would be bound to hesitate before answering. You would be suitably modest and non-committal. But the believer can say with joy and confidence, 'I know I would be accepted if I died tonight. Indeed, I am accepted now, and I have many promises of the New Testament to assure me of it. You see, I am trusting not in anything that I do for acceptance with God, but on what he has done. That is why I can be sure about it. My future is guaranteed by Calvary.'

QUESTIONS

It is at this point that questions flood in. Is the cross all that necessary, you ask? Listen. I had meningitis last year: it is a killer disease. Of course, I did not know I was so ill. I just felt a splitting headache. But when the top physician in Durban came to see me in the middle of a Sunday afternoon and rushed me into hospital, you did not need to persuade me I was ill! If that man had to be called in, I must have been in a serious condition. And if nothing less would suffice than the coming to earth and the death on the cross of Jesus, the Great Physician, then we must have been in a bad way. Do you not think that if there had been any other possible way of rescuing us God would have taken it?

But perhaps you feel that the cross of Christ is unfair. Does it almost seem that God is punishing Jesus instead of us? It is not like that. Actually, the New Testament never speaks of God punishing Jesus on the cross. It does speak of his bearing our sins there. It does speak of his doing so in our place and for our sake. But we must not think of three parties, as it were: God sitting comfortably up in heaven; Jesus in agony on the cross; and you and me going scot free as a result. No. The Bible says that *God* was very much involved in what happened on that cross: God was in Christ, reconciling the world to himself. He was coming in person to deal with the mess we had got ourselves into. It also tells us that *we* were very much involved with what happened there. Jesus was our representative: he was man bearing the consequences of man's rebellion. And just as he died and rose again, so those who come to him have a standing call to share in his death (i.e. allow him to nail our old, sinful nature to the cross, so to speak) and in his resurrection (i.e. allow the power of his risen life to set us free from the ruts of bad habit). Yes, God the Father and we ourselves are very much involved in the cross of Jesus Christ. It would be most misleading and crude to suggest that God 'took it out on' Jesus for us. Rather, he was in Christ on the cross, allowing our rebellion to crush him. Such was his love.

Very well then, what happens to those who have never had a chance to hear the gospel? The New Testament makes it plain that Jesus died not for our sins only but for the sins of the whole world. That death availed for believers who died in ignorance of the cross in the centuries that went before. It availed for the great men of faith in the Old Testament days, men like Abraham and David. They could sing, 'Happy is the man whose iniquity is pardoned and whose sin is covered' because they trusted that God would find a way to do just that. They did not understand how he could, but they trusted in him and not in their own fancied goodness. No doubt it is the same for men after the coming of Jesus who have never heard the gospel — if they genuinely trust in God and not in their own good deeds to save them. The cross was for them, too. And when they hear of it, as they sometimes do through a Bible or a missionary, they rejoice and thank the great God who had found such a marvellous way to settle their debts, grant them pardon and secure their access to him. But that does not let us off the hook, does it? We have heard the message of his love, and what he did for us on the cross. The only proper question is, What are we going to do about it?

'But surely, I don't need to do anything about it?' you may be asking. 'Doesn't the whole thrust of your argument mean that I am automatically forgiven, through what has been done for me on the cross?' Not so. Forgiveness is costly. It always involves two parties. To continue the three analogies we have used about the cross: debts remain unless you cash the cheque you have been given to pay them with. Access may be available, but unless you take it, you remain out of touch with your benefactor. Pardon may be offered: but it has to be accepted. A Royal Pardon offered to some prisoner is quite void until it is accepted. I should be a fool if I ignored it. I should be stupid to take it for granted and assume that naturally I would be entitled to a pardon. I should be mad to say, 'What a beautiful document: I will frame it and use it to decorate the wall of my cell.' I would be out of my mind to tear it up. Obviously, I need to accept it with gratitude and humility. That is just what you need to do with the pardon which God holds out to you in the cross of Jesus Christ. It will do you no good if you take it for granted, or if you say in admiration, 'How wonderful.' It will do you no good if you ignore it all your life. It will do you no good if you tear it up and throw it in the face of the donor. One dying thief was forgiven so that nobody need despair, however bad his past has been, however short his grasp on life. But only one was forgiven, as if to remind us that nobody can dare to presume on the pardon of God, without accepting it personally. The cross of Jesus stands between those two thieves. One was saved, and the other lost. The cross of Jesus is equally divisive in today's world. Some know they are guilty, but know equally that because of what he did on that cross they are forgiven. Others try to pretend that they are all right, and that they do not need pardon, do not need to look to Jesus to change the past. The cross divides those two groups of mankind. Which group do you belong to? Don't rest until you get the matter clear. Mercifully it is possible to move from one group to the other. If a dying thief can discover pardon at the cross, so can you. Don't miss it, for this is the only medicine in the world that can change your guilty past.

9

'*When you're dead,
you're dead!*'

'WHEN I DIE, I rot,' said Bertrand Russell. And you can't argue with that. It is obviously true. But is it the whole truth? Does the real 'me' disappear?

AN INTRIGUING QUESTION

Every few years one of the major daily or Sunday papers takes the matter up. They run a series on 'The great mystery of life after death' or some such title. The insurance companies take it up, with all their loaded advertising about Refuge for Life. The question of life after the grave has intrigued men since the earliest dawn of the human race. I remember seeing some of the oldest tombs in existence at Byblos in the Lebanon. The skeletons were buried in a highly suggestive position. Their knees were tucked up under their chins, and they were encased in an earthenware egg. In other words, the men of that far off day cherished the hope that new life would break out of that egg of death. They hoped that when you were dead you might somehow live again.

I remember being fascinated on a visit to Italy by the preoccupation with this subject among the Romans. There are many mosaics dealing with death and the after-life at Pompeii, the Italian city overwhelmed and buried by the terrible eruption of Vesuvius in A.D. 79. There are pictures of skeletons with jugs in their hands, pictures of death in various guises, and one memorable one of the phoenix, a mythical bird which was supposed to come to life again after it had been burnt on the funeral pyre. Underneath the picture the artist had written, 'Phoenix, how lucky you are!'

To be sure, when you're dead, you're dead. It is very final. There is no return to life. But is it the end of you? Or is there a life beyond? It is a fascinating question.

But there's another side to it.

A THREATENING QUESTION

If there is a life after death, what will it be like? It is bad enough if death is the end, but far worse if it is not. Epicurus, the Greek pleasure-loving philosopher, said long ago, 'What men fear is not that death is annihilation, but that it is not.' And Yeats, in his poem *Death*, catches the feeling precisely:

> Nor dread nor hope attend
> A dying animal.
> A man awaits his end,
> Dreading and hoping all.

What if we shall be called to account for the lives we have lived? What if, as the New Testament puts it, 'it is appointed for all men, once to die, and after that the judgment'; Perish the thought: it would be too awful! But it would be fair, would it not? It would match our freedom. We know all too well that freedom and accountability are the two sides of the same coin. A student has almost unlimited freedom: but the day comes when he has to give an account of it in the final examinations. An architect has enormous freedom in designing and building a house. But at the end of the day he is accountable to his employer. What if life is like that? What if it should be true that 'every one of us shall give an account of himself to God'?

What if Jesus was right in his story of the rich fool? The man lived as though this life was all there is; he made success and money and property his gods, and left God out. And then, one night he died. God said to him, 'You fool, tonight your life will be required of you. And then who will come in for all that property you will have to leave behind?' A devastating story, very apt for our materialistic age. Could Jesus be right? If so, it would not be much fun to have God saying 'You fool' to you. I saw an advertisement for life assurance not long ago, advising me to invest in the company, and ending with this sardonic note: 'Let those who think they are going to live for ever make their own arrangements.' What if we do live on — and have not made any arrangements?

What if Jesus is right in his story of the rich man and Lazarus? What if there is a life after the grave and we are accountable for the way we have lived in this one? For our selfishness, our callous disregard of the needs of the Lazaruses on our doorstep, not to mention the half of the world's population who live on the bread line because of economic policies pursued by the greedy West? What if we shall be judged in that day by the way we have treated the coloured bus driver, the dustman, or the old person in the senile ward of the local hospital? Of course, prejudice, including racism, is two-way. One black Christian leader challenged his fellow blacks recently like this. 'At the judgment day, the Lord will say to us, "Why didn't you preach the gospel to all those poor whites lost in affluence and ambition?" ' What if such an unpalatable possibility turned out to be true after all?

'Ah,' you say, 'it is all sheer speculation. How can you possibly know?'

A QUESTION THAT CAN BE ANSWERED

One could only know if there is a life beyond the grave if someone came back with reliable information. And that is, by definition, impossible. Dead men don't rise. When you're dead, you're dead. But this brings us to the very heart of the Christian claim. Alone among the religions of the world it dares to maintain that we can know about life after death, we can know how to get there, we can know something of what awaits us, for one simple and sufficient reason, that Jesus Christ, crucified on the cross, rose again from the grave.

Now this is a preposterous claim. It cannot be true. Or can it? There is, of course, only one way of finding out whether there is a life beyond the grave or not. And that would be for someone to die and come back to tell us what it is like. I suppose it's a bit like space exploration. The moon has fascinated mankind from time immemorial. Was there, or was there not life on this mysterious world of the moon? What were conditions like on the side of the moon we cannot see? Nobody could tell, though that did not stop lots of guessing. Nobody could tell until Neil Armstrong, the first man to land on the moon, came back to tell us what it is like. Not only that, but he paved the way for later space travellers to follow.

THE CHRISTIAN CLAIM

Now that is precisely how the Christian claim about life after death can be assessed. We believe that one man, Jesus of Nazareth, came back from beyond the grave to show us that he has overcome the last enemy and to enable us to follow in his footsteps. Of course we know that dead men are not in the habit of rising from their tombs. We know that there is no scientifically established category of dead men who come back to life again. We are not naïve: we know that this claim makes the imagination boggle. But we believe it all the same, and on good evidence. I will give you some of that evidence in a moment. But just now let's be clear abut one thing. We are not making this claim for any old Tom, Dick or Harry. We are maintaining that in one man, one very special man, one who was more than man, the forces of death met their match. We saw in chapter 5 strong reasons for supposing that Jesus was no less God than man. How can we be dogmatic that he could not rise from the grave in that case? We saw that he lived an absolutely unspoiled and perfect life. How can we be so sure that a life which has given no foothold to sin could not master death? We have no other to compare it with. Jesus made his whole credibility rest upon the assertion that he would 'do a Jonah' on his contemporaries, and just as Jonah came back from his three day 'death' inside the great fish, so he himself would rise from the jaws of death (Matthew 12: 39–41). So let us lay aside blind prejudice that says 'It couldn't happen', and see whether, according to all the evidence, it *did* happen in this one solitary case of Jesus. If he was perfect man, if he was more than man, we cannot rule it out of court.

I have tried to look at the evidence in some detail in a little book *Man Alive*. You might care to follow the matter up there. But here are five points to consider, as you reflect on the events of that first Good Friday.

1. THE MAN WAS DEAD

Very dead. Roman executions were grimly thorough. As a matter of fact, the officer in charge of the execution was himself liable to the death penalty if his job was not done efficiently. In the case of Jesus, the execution squad saw that he was dead already, and so did not bother to break his legs (a barbaric way of ensuring the crucified wretches did not continue to raise themselves on their crosses and gulp in breath). But just to make doubly sure, they pierced his side with a spear, and out came 'blood and water' as an eyewitness put it (John 19: 34f). This is a fascinating detail, all the more remarkable because the writer could have no idea of its medical significance. But any doctor now will tell you that the separation of the blood into clot and serum is one of the surest indications of death. That is what St. John records, even though he could only marvel at it, not understand it. But it gives proof positive that Jesus was dead. If we wanted more, we could have it: not only did the centurion report to the governor that the job was done (and he knew a dead man when he saw one — he had despatched enough of them), but Pilate himself allowed Joseph of Arimathea to take the body away (John 19: 38). It is another fascinating touch to discover that the word here used for 'body' of Jesus is, in the original Greek 'corpse': the word is never used of a live man, always of a dead one.

Yes, Jesus was dead all right. So any variety of the 'swoon theory' that suggests Jesus recovered from his terrible ordeal in the cool of the tomb, and crept out, is utterly discredited. It simply couldn't have happened. But so keen have unbelievers been to reject the plain teaching of the New Testament writers (based though it is on eyewitness testimony), that they have had recourse to theories which maintain that Jesus was not really dead. You find it as long ago as Celsus in the second century. He was a strong anti-Christian who explained the resurrection by supposing that Jesus was nursed back to health again by Mary Magdalene: forty days later his wounds got the better of him, and he died and was buried secretly, but not before he had assembled his friends and walked off into a cloud on a mountain top! Such poverty stricken explanations are still put forward from time to time, recently in Hugh Schonfield's *The Passover Plot*. They are wrecked on the massive evidence that Jesus was indeed dead. They are also psychologically inprobable in the extreme. Would disciples who knew that Jesus was not risen from the tomb but he had died ignominiously from his wounds, have gone all over the world proclaiming his risen presence with such joy that men felt they might be drunk, and with such persistence that prison, torture and death could not stop them? You don't let yourself be bumped off for a fraud . . .

2. THE TOMB WAS EMPTY

Very empty, on that first Easter morning. And nobody has ever been able to suggest a really plausible explanation, apart from the united testimony of every strand in the New Testament that the tomb was empty because Jesus had conquered death and was alive again.

Of course, people have had a go at explaining it away. One distinguished professor suggested that in the mist of early dawn Mary and her friends found the wrong tomb! Did she not do better later, we might ask? Was Joseph of Arimathea equally clueless on the location of his own personal tomb which he had given over to Jesus? Another crude suggestion, made as early as the end of the second century, has at least a touch of humour about it. It suggests that the gardner was responsible for all the talk about the resurrection of Jesus. He was so fed up at sightseers stumping around the tomb, treading all over the seedlings he had planted out, that he removed the body and buried it elsewhere! Another rationalisation of the empty tomb appears in the New Testament itself. The soldiers, set to guard the tomb were bribed by the embarrassed Jews to explain the absence of the body of Jesus by asserting that they fell asleep, and then the disciples of Jesus came and stole his body (Matthew 28: 11–15).

But all these attempts to explain away the empty tomb on the assumption that someone stole the body come unstuck very fast, on this simple point. There were only two lots of people interested in what became of the body of this executed teacher: his friends and his enemies. The records all show us that his friends had no idea that he might rise; they were not expecting anything of the sort. Rather, they scattered sadly like any other band whose hopes had been dashed by the death of their leader. There was no expectation in Judaism that any prophet or teacher might personally come back from the grave, though

there was the hope of a general resurrection at the Last Day.
His disciples were not expecting his resurrection. What's more,
if they had been able to spirit the body away (despite the strict
guard kept on the tomb), they would scarcely have been prepared to die for their fraud: nor would people all over the world
and in all generations from then till now be so confident that
Jesus lives.

But if it was not the disciples who stole the body, how could
it have been the opposition? They had been working for his
execution for ages. And now it had come about. The last thing
they would have done is to give colour to any talk about resurrection by moving his body surreptitiously. They had got him
where they wanted, dead and buried. We may be sure they
spared no effort to keep him there — hence the seal and the
guard on the tomb. To suggest that either the Jews or the
Romans moved his body is a beggar's refuge from having to
admit the truth of the resurrection. Had they been so incredibly
foolish, they would only have had to produce the body of Jesus
when the disciples claimed his resurrection, in order to squash
the new movement at a single stroke. And this is what nobody
was able to do. They just got very cross with the apostles, tried
to silence them, put them in prison, tortured and killed them.
But they could not discredit their story, that the tomb was
empty because Jesus was risen.

Did you ever notice the fascinating bit of corroborative
detail in St. John's account of the resurrection? He tells with
artless simplicity of Peter and the beloved disciple racing to the
sepulchre to see for themselves after Mary had brought them
the incredible news that Jesus was alive. When they got to the
tomb, they stooped down, looked in, and saw the linen ban-
dages that had been wound round Jesus' body, intertwined with
spices (the Eastern way of burial) lying wrapped up ... but
with nobody inside. They saw the turban which had been
wound round his head 'not lying with the linen clothes, but
wrapped together in a place by itself' (John 20: 7). At that
point, we read, they saw and believed. Why? Because it was
apparent to them that the body of Jesus had emerged from

those graveclothes, just as a butterfly emerges from its chrysalis: and the turban lay apart, just like the cap of a chrysalis
case when the butterfly has come out. Incidentally, this has
something to say about the modern suggestion that the resurrection of Jesus was somehow real but not physical. That seems
to me rather like trying to have your cake and eat it. To be sure,
Christians have never held that the resurrection of Jesus was
the mere resuscitation of a corpse. The New Testament pro-
claims that he was raised to a life of a new quality. Just like the
butterfly, in fact. It does not emerge unchanged from when it
went into that chrysalis. No, it is transformed to a new dimension of living. No longer is it a caterpillar which crawls
slowly and painfully wherever it wants to go. Now it can sail
through the air with delicacy and poise. It is freed into another
element in its new life. But it is unquestionably the same insect,
despite the change brought about by its hibernation in the chrysalis. So it was with Jesus. His tomb was not empty in order to
let him out; but to let men in to see that he had indeed risen.
The empty tomb and the empty graveclothes are symbols,
pointers, to the fact that Jesus, the man, has become Christ, the
risen Lord. 'He holds the keys of death and of the after life,'
sang the prophet who wrote the Book of Revelation (1: 17).
The man was indeed dead. But the tomb was found empty because death could not hold him. And that, as Peter said on the
first Day of Pentecost, was a remarkable fulfilment of a
prophecy made a thousand years beforehand:

> David says, concerning Jesus, 'Thou wilt not abandon my
> soul to Hades, nor let thy Holy One see corruption. Thou has
> made known to me the ways of life . . .' Brethren, I may say
> to you confidently of the patriarch David that he both
> died and was buried, and his tomb is with us to this day . . .
> But being a prophet he foresaw the resurrection of Christ,
> that he was not abandoned to Hades, nor did his flesh see cor-
> ruption. This Jesus God raised up, and of that we are all
> witnesses (Acts 2: 25–32).

3. THE CHURCH WAS BORN

In a fascinating and most penetrating study, *The Phenomenon of the New Testament*, Professor C. F. D. Moule, points out a very remarkable thing about Christianity. It had absolutely nothing to add to Judaism, nothing whatsoever — except this conviction that the Rabbi Jesus had been raised from the dead! All the earliest Christians were loyal Jews, of course. They all went to the synagogue to worship. They read and believed the Jewish Scriptures. Their ethics were based on the Old Testament. Only one thing caused this new religion (as it became) to erupt. It was the conviction that Jesus must be the long awaited Deliverer from God, foretold in those Scriptures of the Old Testament, hinted at in all the sacrificial ceremonial of the Jewish people. He must be the Coming One; his resurrection from the dead proved it (Romans 1: 4). Nobody else had done that. Jesus was unique. No wonder they could do no less than give him the title 'Lord', the name usually applied to Almighty God in the Old Testament Scriptures.

That church, armed with such an improbable claim, swept across the whole Roman Empire inside three hundred years. It is a perfectly amazing story of peaceful revolution, without parallel in the history of the world. It came about because Christians were able to say to unbelievers, 'Jesus did not only die for you, but is alive. You can meet him, and discover for yourself the reality we are talking about.' People did discover for themselves. And the church, born out of the Easter grave, spread.

That church had three special characteristics. You found them everywhere it went. The Christians had a special day, Sunday; a special rite of initiation, baptism; and a special meal, the Holy Communion. Now the interesting thing about that fact is this. Every one of the three is rooted in the resurrection of Jesus. Sunday, called 'the Lord's Day' in Revelation 1: 10, was given this remarkable name because it was the day, the first day of the week, on which the Lord Jesus rose from the tomb. The Jews had, from time immemorial, kept the

seventh day of the week sacred. It recalled the completion of
God's work of creation. Indeed, its observance was laid down in
the Ten Commandments, and remains one of the most dis-
tinguishing features of the Jewish nation. Yet these Jews who
knew that Jesus was risen reckoned, reasonably enough, that
God's new creation in the resurrection of Christ was even more
memorable and significant than his act of creating the world
in the first instance. It is quite something to change the day of
rest after several thousand years. It needed nothing less than
the resurrection to trigger it off.

Then there was Christian baptism. You went down into a
river, repenting of your sins, and professing your faith in Jesus
as Saviour and Lord. You were immersed. You climbed out the
other side. What did it mean? Simply this. That you, as a
disciple, were linked to your Lord who went down into the dark
river of death *and came up the other side.* It was an initiation
ceremony which would have been unthinkable apart from the
resurrection of Jesus.

It was just the same with the Lord's Supper, as they called it.
This simple meal of bread and wine was shared by the Christians in memory of Jesus' body broken (like the loaf) for them,
and his blood poured out (like the wine) for them. Understandable enough. But when the New Testament writers talk
about this meal as an opportunity for exultant gladness, we can
see that it is more than a memorial meal for a departed hero.
They believed that the Lord who had died was alive and present in their midst. Death itself was conquered, and the
Conqueror was with them in all his risen power.

Baptism, Communion, Sunday, all point to that resurrection
of Jesus from the grave which acted as a launching pad — the
only launching pad — for the whole Christian rocket which
burst upon the ancient world.

4. THE LORD APPEARED

Quite unmistakably. To lots of people. St. Paul gives a list of
some of them in 1 Corinthians 15, a letter he wrote about

twenty years after the event, when plenty of eyewitnesses were still alive. Curiously enough he does not mention the appearance of Jesus to Mary of Magdala, though all the Gospels are clear that she was the first witness of the resurrection. Perhaps this was because no woman was considered a proper witness in either Jewish or Gentile law in ancient society. Incidentally, if Christians had dreamed up the story of the empty tomb, would they have been stupid enough to attribute the discovery of that tomb and the first sight of the risen Jesus to a woman, whose testimony was legally worthless? That fact alone speaks volumes for the truth of the resurrection story. Although there were plenty of men who saw him later, it was to a despised woman that Jesus first appeared. Somehow it seems typical of him.

Let's glance at this list of witnesses which Paul brings us in 1 Corinthians 15. 'I deliver to you as of first importance what I also received,' he says to the men of Corinth — incidentally using the words 'delivered' and 'received' in their technical sense of passing on duly authorised facts. What did he pass on? 'Christ died for our sins according to the Scriptures. He was buried. He was raised on the third day according to the Scriptures, and he appeared . . .' To whom? First in the list he mentions Peter, the Peter who had denied him. Then 'the twelve', presumably excluding Judas (dead) and Thomas (absent). Then he appeared to more than five hundred Christians at once, probably in Galilee where the majority of his followers lived. 'Most of them are still alive,' adds Paul: as if to say, you can go and check up on the resurrection with them if you like. Jesus then appeared to James, his brother. He appeared to 'all the apostles', presumably including Thomas this time. He appeared also to Paul. Now put together that lot: women, fishermen, a sceptical brother, a fanatical Pharisee opponent, and five hundred ordinary folk. Can any theory of hallucination cover those appearances? Hallucinations tend to happen to particular types of people — no one type here. Hallucinations tend to be allied with wish fulfilment — none of that here. Hallucinations tend to recur. These appearances ended after forty days and never came again. Hallucinations belong to the sick world — and it is hard to maintain that there was anything sick about these early missionaries as they preached the full health and salvation that their risen Messiah brought them. No, these appearances of the risen Christ are without parallel in the religious history of mankind. Nowhere else do you find anybody, still less so great a diversity of people claiming to have had intimate personal contact (even to go as far as eating fish and honeycomb) with a much loved leader recently killed. And it will not do to suppose that these were mere subjective visions. At least one of the apostles, Paul, was accustomed to having visions, was proud of them, and was very sure that this appearance of the Risen One was no vision (1 Corinthians 9: 1, 2 Corinthians 12: 1ff.) It was real.

5. THEIR LIVES WERE CHANGED ...

This has always been one of the strongest proofs of the truth of the resurrection. Those who claim to have come in touch with the risen Christ have had their lives transformed. Think of that list we looked at just now. Peter was changed from a coward who denied and forsook his Master when the crunch came, into a man of rock whom the Establishment could not cow by dint of threats, imprisonment or death sentence. Think of the twelve, who were transformed from defeatists into a task force by the resurrection: theirs is one of the greatest 'come-back' stories in the world. The five hundred were changed from a rabble into a church. All the apostles, including Thomas, came from unbelief to ardent faith. James, Jesus' sceptical brother, becomes suddenly changed into a believer, and more, the leader of the Jerusalem church: a fantastic turn-up for the book. What accounts for it? Simple: 'he appeared to James'. And perhaps most amazing of all is that volte-face of Saul of Tarsus, the violent, bigoted persecutor of the Christians, into the greatest follower Jesus ever had. The reason? 'Last of all, he appeared to me.'

... AND STILL ARE

But that first century stuff is only half the story, remarkable
though it is. It is not quite the same since those days, because
nobody has seen the risen Lord with his own eyes. I imagine
that Jesus displayed himself openly to his followers, allowed
them to feel the holes in his hands and feet, even ate meals
with them, in order to persuade them that he was still the Jesus
they had known. Yet he passed through doors, disappeared
while they were talking with him, and eventually parted from
them for the last time on the Mount of Olives in order to persuade them that he had risen not just to a further span of life,
but to a new quality of life. From then on he would not
appear to their physical eyes. But by his Spirit, no longer restricted to the confines of a physical body, he would indwell the
very lives of his people, not just be alongside them, as he had
during his time on earth. And that is what he has been doing
ever since. So although we cannot say, like the first witnesses, 'I
have seen the Lord,' every genuine Christian can say 'I know
him. He has come into my life. He has made such radical
changes that I cannot believe I am kidding myself.' Every believer is, in this sense, a witness of the resurrection.

This, to me, was the most impressive demonstration of the
truth that Jesus is alive. I watched the lives of Christians for
the best part of a year, and I discovered them to be
different — different from my own, and different from what
they had been. The other day I was having a discussion with a
number of post-graduate scientists, and you can imagine the
number of objections to Christianity which were coming forward. And then one of the agnostics said simply, 'I know there
must be something in it because of the difference it has made to
my friends.'

The life-changing work of the risen Jesus goes on today, and
it is a powerful testimony to the truth that he is indeed alive
and well. I have been a Christian long enough now to be sure
that I am not kidding myself. I have seen Christ's transforming
touch change obviously needy characters, like long-term pris-

oners, compulsive gamblers and alcoholics, drug addicts and prostitutes. I am just as moved by the way he changes attitudes and character in more ordinary people. I think of a brilliant athlete I have known for only six weeks. He also has a brilliant political career ahead of him. He was intensely ambitious. But now he is quite clear that his games are to be used as a talent from God, and that his political career is in the Master's hands and is to be used for His glory, not for the satisfaction of his own ambition. The peace, the relaxation that has come to him through allowing the Risen One to take over, is remarkable. His friends are noticing it.

Or I think of an Oxford student I have known for a similar time. I met her first in church, when she was wrestling against the Christ she had become convinced was real. It was a long and tearful fight. Eventually she gave in. Now she is not only a very different character, more gracious, more outgoing, more thoughtful of others, but she is going to give up two weeks of her vacation in going on a mission to share with others the discovery she has herself made. No matter whether it is in a spectacular conversion, or far more gentle ways, the risen Christ shines through his present day witnesses. It reminds me a bit of the ending of *Godspell*. In this musical the joy of the resurrection is shown through dance. And members of the audience are invited to come up on to the stage and dance with the cast. They do not thereby become the cast, but they share the same experience. Now the cast, so to speak, is the first generation of disciples: Peter, James and John and others who saw the risen Christ. We cannot join that cast of eyewitnesses. But we can join them in the dance of Christian experience, if we have come to know the living Lord.

THE IMPLICATIONS

Those, then, are five pieces of evidence. Together they point to one conclusion, that Jesus of Nazareth did not only die but rose to a new life, an endless life, which enables him to meet and transform character today — your character, even — just as he did in the first century. We can be confident that Jesus pioneered the way through death, just as those first astronauts pioneered the way to the moon. And just as they brought back evidence about what lay on the hidden side of the moon, so he has shown what lies on the hidden side of death. Death is not the end. It is, or it can be, the gateway into a new quality of life, 'butterfly life' instead of 'caterpillar life'.

If this is the case, we would be wise to listen very carefully to what this pioneer, Jesus, has to say about the hidden side of death. He ought to know. He has been there. He is very explicit. 'Let not your hearts be troubled,' he says to his disciples, grief-stricken at the prospect of his death, 'believe in God, believe also in me. In my Father's house there are many rooms. If it were not so I would have told you. I go to prepare a place for you' (John 14: 1ff). Those are words we can trust. They come from the one person who has broken the death barrier, the one person equipped to take other colonists with him to that uncharted land.

But there is another side of the coin. It is true that the Christian can be confident that God will not scrap him at death. It is true he can rest with assurance on this promise of Jesus. He can look forward to death not as the end, but as the end of the caterpillar stage. But what of the man who is not linked to the Risen One? How can he hope to fare? Not very well, obviously. I should not fare very well if I tried to get to the moon under my own steam, however much hardware and rocketry was put at my disposal. I should need the skilled direction of an astronaut who had done it before. Without that, I should not stand a chance. That is why Jesus said to people who turned their backs on him, 'I go away, and you will seek me and die in your sin. Where I am going you cannot come' (John 8: 21). Does that sound hard? Not really. You cannot get to the moon unless you commit yourself to the astronaut. It is very sad, though. Jesus grieved over people who turned down his offer of life abundant, life for ever. 'You refuse to come to me that you may have life' (John 5: 40). Curiously enough, the practical answer to the riddle of whether or not there is a life beyond the grave lies with us. We may choose whether when we die we rot; or whether death becomes for us the chrysalis case to usher in a new quality of life with the Risen One.

10

'You can't change human nature'

BY AND LARGE, you can't change human nature. That is why the early years are so important. The influence of home and school, of first years in the job or time at university, tend to form our main characteristics. They will change to some extent with fresh opportunities, new pressures, responsibility (or the lack of it), and age. But once the direction of a man's life and character are set, you do not find that rapid changes of character and attitude occur very often. You have only to think of the married couple whose years of living with one another enable them to predict with painful accuracy how the partner will react, even what he will say, in a given situation. Or think of the man who comes out of prison only to return there again for a similar offence. Only this morning I heard on the radio of a man convicted of selling goods supposedly made by and for the benefit of the blind: he was now out of prison, and was a director of a firm selling goods supposedly made by and for the benefit of old age pensioners! The leopard does not very often change his spots. You can indeed train up a young tree, or a young dog for that matter, in the direction that you want. But try bending a mature tree; try training a five-year-old dog, and you will be in for disappointment.

Solzhenitsyn put the problem with his customary clarity, 'Human nature changes not much faster than the geological face of the earth.' Indeed, the irony and the tragedy of modern life lies in this: we have become masters of our environment to a very large degree, but cannot produce any comparable control over ourselves. We can alter environment but not people. Of course, we have had a good try.

POSSIBLE REMEDIES?

Political and social liberation has been one greatly favoured avenue of change. Throw out the colonial regime and all will be well. It can scarcely be argued that the result has lived up to the expectation. As I write India is being subjected to curtailment of liberty greater than anything faced in Imperial days. Nigeria seemed to be the ideal of a country peacefully passing from colonial rule to independence — but since then has suffered a disastrous civil war on tribal and financial issues, has refused to return from military to civilian rule, and has thrown out its head of state, while corruption continues unhindered. Do you feel, 'We don't do things that way in the West.' No? But think of the promises offered by political parties at elections, and how ragged and moth-eaten those high hopes seem a year or so later. Political liberation does not change human nature. Neither does the permissiveness of social liberation. Bertrand Russell, one of the foremost advocates of permissiveness in his generation, said with feeling about his own children at the end of his life, 'To let children go free was to establish a reign of terror.' And that is just what is happening in many schools today.

It would be tiresome to multiply examples. Patent remedies for ailing humanity have included education, the Welfare State and psychological medicine. None of these have had more than a marginal effect on the basic problem of changing human nature. Education is more and more non-directional these days, and the same is true of counselling. This is good in so far as it allows a man to find his own resources in himself; but it doesn't help when that same man finds himself to be his prison. Psychological medicine can no more infuse any new element into human nature than education can. And yet human nature cries out for change. Many millions of pounds a year are spent in Britain on pills, sleeping tablets and the like to relieve tension, depression and insomnia. Hundreds of thousands in Britain die every year as a result of the two most common analgesic drugs, tobacco and alcohol. The Welfare State cannot eradicate these human problems. Indeed, in some ways it encourages them to fester. I know unemployed people who will not work because it pays them better to be on unemployment pay and social security. I know students who regard it as their right to fritter away their time at university, rather than treating it responsibly as a privilege for which other people are paying. And there have been more than enough examples of fraud, corruption, avarice, deceit and cruelty under Socialist and Communist administrations to convince most of us that however many benefits we owe to a socialist Welfare State, there is one thing it cannot do: change human nature.

The problem is indeed intractable. Look at unhappiness in the work forces of the world, due to rival policies of greed and lack of job satisfaction. Look at unhappiness in so many homes, due to various brands of selfishness. Look at the tense relationships between many nations, due to rival policies of threat and

hate. Look at the ecological situation, with its ruthless pur-
suance of short-term goals and neglect of future generations.
Wherever you look, you see the ravages of the 'human disease'.
We all have been infected by it. We do not have to learn to go
wrong, though we do have to learn, painfully and slowly, to go
right. To steal and lie, to clamour for our own way, to hate and
lust, to be greedy and selfish are not imported products. They
grow here, in you and me. And they grow with the perverse
fecundity of weeds in our gardens: they need no planting, no
watering, no care — whereas the flowers have to be cosseted and
looked after with tender loving care if they are to survive, let
alone bloom. The human disease is like that very troublesome
weed, ground elder. The more you pull it up, the more it seems
to grow. Leave one particle of root in the soil, and it produces a
fertile crop of the weed in next to no time. Nothing seems able
to eradicate it. And so it is with the human disease. Nothing
seems able to eradicate it, and so we give up trying, and say,
'You can't change human nature.'

DISASTROUS REMEDIES?

Of course, some things *can* change it. Brain operations can do
this, and alter the personality of the patient beyond recognition.
Brainwashing can, so much so that the captive can be trained
actually to think like the captor. And perhaps disaster can.
There are instances where the death of a close relative or the
collapse of a love affair has changed a person's personality and
whole outlook on life enormously. But all three of these pos-
sibilities, disaster, brainwashing and brain surgery we instinc-
tively class as bad things. The cure is worse than the disease. If
human nature can only be changed at the dictates of brain sur-
geons with their scalpels, brainwashers with their instruments
of refined torture, and personal disasters, it is a pretty grim
lookout. For all practical purposes we can say again, 'You can't
change human nature.'

There is nothing new about this conclusion. Thinkers and
poets all down the ages have recognised it. Herodotus, the

father of history, commented on it. Plato, the greatest philosopher there has ever been, discovered the hard truth of it
when he tried to educate the tyrant of Syracuse. For all his
educative theory and unsurpassed skill as a teacher, he failed
miserably, and was ejected for his pains by that unpleasant
youth. Ovid, the poet, banished by the Emperor Augustus for
his eroticism, combined realism and humour as he wrote, 'I see
the better course, and I approve of it: but I follow the worse.'
Those words were echoed by his contemporary, St. Paul. He
spoke of the miserable human condition which he shared. 'I
don't understand myself at all, for I really want to do what is
right, but I can't. I do what I don't want to — what I hate. I . . .
know I am rotten through and through so far as my old sinful
nature is concerned. No matter which way I turn I can't make
myself do right. I want to but I can't. I want to do good, but
when I try not to do wrong, I do it anyway . . .'

Doesn't that first century rabbi speak to your condition?
Isn't it just like that with you? It is with me. Very well then,
might it not be worth listening to his momentous claim, since
his analysis of our human disease is so convincing? His claim is
simply this: that there is a cure. That he had found it and
applied it, and discovered that it did change his human nature,
but in a way far different from the grim effects of the brain
surgery, the brainwashing, and the disasters we have considered.
As you would expect with this redoubtable opponent of the
Man of Nazareth who became his foremost apostle and
preacher, this cure all centres round Jesus. May I recap a little
at this stage in the book?

EFFECTIVE REMEDY?

We have seen that the really conclusive answer to whether there
is a God or not is Jesus Christ. He is the embodiment of that
invisible divinity in terms we could understand, human terms.
He brings us all of God we could take in. He was not just a
good man, he was God himself joining his nature to ours, and
coming on to the floor of our factory, so to speak. All religions

point to a dimension higher than our own. All have within them some search for the truth. All possess some elements of the light which has taken full and final form in the Light of the World, Jesus Christ himself. So God himself has met one of our basic needs, to know about himself. He has come to show us.

We have another basic need, to get right with this God who has shown his loveliness of character, his goodness and fierce hatred of evil, in Jesus. If God is Christlike, it is very plain that I am not. And there lies a problem. We considered it in chapter 7. No good deeds from me, no payment, no religious activities could span the yawning gulf between the Lord's goodness and my — let's be frank about it — my badness. This problem was so acute that it led to the cross. It directed Jesus inexorably to the place where he laid down his life for ours, where he took responsibility for all man's evil in the sight of God. Such was God's generosity that Jesus did not merely come to show us what he was like, but he died that most agonising death to reconcile us, and enable anyone who was prepared to say 'God be merciful to me, a sinner' to enjoy his company here on earth, and also (this is one of the important sides to the resurrection which we considered in chapter 9) hereafter.

All these things St. Paul writes about in his letters which are preserved in our New Testament. He rejoices in them; he is thrilled by them. He is completely taken up in loving adoration and service of the God who makes them available. But there is one other side in this all-embracing rescue which God has done for us, that thrills Paul almost more than any of the others. It is this. God has found a way to change human nature.

THE SPIRIT OF JESUS

Briefly, what it amounts to is this. He is willing not just to reveal himself to us, not merely to die for us. He is actually prepared to come and live in us. Now if that sounds stupid, wait a moment. We get somewhere near it when in ordinary speech we say, 'Stalin had the spirit of Hitler in him,' or that 'Jimmy is a proper Don Juan.' We mean that the sort of qualities found in Hitler or Don Juan are reproduced in Stalin or Jimmy. Well, that includes what a Christian means when he speaks of Christ's Spirit coming to live in him. We mean that the same characteristics that were seen in Jesus begin to make their appearance in the lives of his followers. Paul put it like this. He said, 'When the Holy Spirit controls our lives he will produce this kind of fruit in us: love, joy, peace, patience, kindness, goodness, faithfulness, gentleness and self-control' (Galatians 5: 22). But Christians mean a lot more than this. We mean that this Jesus who died and rose is not a spent force. He is alive and well. When he was here in Palestine he was limited in what he could do and where he could be. If he was talking to me here, he could not be talking to you there. Such are the limitations of the human body. But shortly before his death Jesus told his followers that it would be a good thing for them if he went away; if he did not, the Spirit would not become available for them. If he did go, however, he would send the Spirit in his place to make his presence real to them. And that was precisely what they experienced.

It all began on the Day of Pentecost, just fifty days after the crucifixion of Jesus Christ at Passover time. To their amazement they had, many of them, seen the risen Jesus during those intervening weeks. They had become convinced that he was vibrantly alive. The Risen One told them that these appearances of his were only temporary, and that as a permanent gift his Spirit would come and indwell their very personalities. They did not understand what he meant, despite Old Testament Scriptures which spoke of God putting his Spirit within his followers, and enabling them each to know him and to walk in his ways. But after their experience on the Day of Pentecost, they knew for sure. They had a living experience of the Spirit of Jesus not merely influencing them from outside, but coming to grow the lovely flowers of his character in the barren soil of their own lives. They were, quite literally, born into a new dimension of experience, as a foetus is when it struggles through the birth canal and draws its first breath, or as a woman does the day she gets married, or a larva the day it turns into a dragon fly. The natural world does prepare us, just a little, for the truth that human nature can be changed by the renewing power of the Holy Spirit of God, once he is accepted into our lives. And this realisation gives the Christian something to sing about. After that heartrending cry of defeat from Paul the un-aided human being, which we saw above, Paul the Christian can proclaim triumphantly, 'There is now no condemnation await-ing those who belong to Christ Jesus. For the power of the lifegiving Spirit — and this power is mine through Jesus Christ — has freed me from the vicious circle of sin and death … So now we can obey God's laws if we are led by the Holy Spirit and no longer obey the old evil nature within us' (Romans 8:1ff).

In the remainder of this chapter I propose to glance at ten practical examples, taken from the pages of the New Tes-tament or from contemporary experience, of what the Holy Spirit can do in a man, once he is given control.

1. CHANGED ATTITUDES

First, the Spirit of Jesus can change your inner attitudes. I can't combat my own deep-seated prejudices. But the Spirit of the God who made me and died to reconcile me, can do just that. I remember a saintly missionary, Bishop Don Jacobs, tell-ing of a dream he had shortly after beinning work as a white man in a black African area. He still retained some illusions about white superiority, and his work was, not unnaturally, hampered by this. In the dream he saw himself on a hot day standing by a river in which many native people were washing themselves. 'Go and bathe, Don,' the Lord's Spirit seemed to be saying to him. 'Not beneath all those folk, Lord,' was his instinctive response: 'I'll swim upstream of them.' And then he saw in his dream that the river welled out from the cross of Calvary. There was no room for pride of place there. So he gladly immersed himself in that river, downstream of his Afri-can brethren, and on that day the Spirit of God dealt with his inbred arrogance. Thereafter for many years of loving ministry among African peoples there was no hint of pride in his dealings with them. He was a new man: his very attitudes had been changed.

2. LIFESTYLE ALTERED

Second, the Spirit of Jesus can change your whole way of life. It may or may not have been socially acceptable previously; but it needed attention. I think of two eminently respectable people, a mother of four, and a leading civic official. The mother's sharpness with the children, impatience with the chores, and less than kind gossip has changed radically: people wonder what has happened to her. The official's attitude to his subordinates, once overbearing, is now gracious; his love of money has been taken away, and he now sees his possessions as a trust to use for God. But I think also of one not so respectable — a hospital porter who came to Christ at much the same time as these two. He had committed a long list of crimes which had never been detected. What did the Spirit of God prompt him to do? Something that he would never have dreamed of doing of his own accord: to go and confess his crimes to the police. This he did — and they were very surprised! In both 'respectable' and 'unacceptable' the Spirit of Christ was altering lifestyle.

The delightful thing about this transformation is that it is basically the same wherever men and women come to Christ. The Spirit of the risen Lord begins to change their lives for the better, and gradually make them more like Christ. It was so in the first days of the church. Think of those disciples who wanted to burn down a Samaritan village just because they got a cold welcome there in the days that Jesus was with them. A few years later, after they had received his Spirit into their lives, they were spreading the gospel of love and forgiveness to those same Samaritans. Some of the earliest converts, the Thessalonians, who turned from idols to the true God, showed it in the way they lived: Paul can commend them on their increase in faith and love, the holiness that was replacing lust, the hu-

mility that replaced their traditional Macedonian arrogance,
and their patience in suffering and persecution. Last year I met
a man from an animist background like theirs. He was a head-
man among the Naga tribesmen who live in the mountains of
India. Large-scale conversions to Christ have been taking place
there recently. His aim used previously to be to gain his
enemy's scalp. Now it is to present to that same enemy the love
of the Spirit of Jesus which has taken over his own personality
with such evident radiance.

3. HABITS BROKEN

Third, the Spirit of Jesus can break long standing habits. Of
course he can: Jesus was never bound by habits he could not
control, and 'where the Spirit of the Lord is, there is liberty'. A
friend of mine has been inside many of the borstals and prisons
in England, for stealing cars. He found Christ while serving a
sentence in one of those prisons, and has never been back. His
philosophy of 'Get from no matter whom' has changed to 'Give
to no matter whom', and he is now in the ordained ministry of
the Church of England. He does not have much money now,
but he is content. Like St Paul of old, he has found that the lifegiving power of the Spirit of Jesus has set him free from the
vicious circle of the old ways.

This sort of thing is not the exception once the Spirit of
Christ gets inside a man; it becomes the rule. I think of an
obsessive gambler set free from his craze to gamble. I think of
chain smokers, knowing their habit to be harmful but unable to
break it, who welcomed the Spirit of Christ into their lives, and
discovered the reality of his power to snap the habit. I think of
folk who could scarcely utter a sentence without an oath, whose
long standing habit was broken by the Spirit of Jesus. It is not
only with the famous people and the great sins that the Spirit of
Jesus can help. The Spirit, endued with all the power of the
risen Lord Jesus, is meant for *you*.

4. LOVE FOR HATE

Fourth, the Spirit of Jesus can replace hate by love. Hate is one of the two most powerful human emotions, and love is the other. Although in some ways they are very near to one another, so that a lover, once jilted, can passionately hate the person he once loved, you don't very often find it happening the other way round. But the Spirit of Jesus makes a habit of it. I have seen the faces of black South Africans filled with joy and love for white brother Christians who belong to the race of those who have oppressed them. I have seen the love of Biafran Christians towards Nigerian Christians during and after the war. I have seen the absence of resentment and sheer caring generosity shine out from the Kenyan Christians tortured by their fellow Kenyans in the Mau Mau risings. I think of the love of those missionaries who in the late 1950s went to try to evangelise the savage stone-age tribe of the Aucas in South America, and got speared to death for their pains. Their wives and sisters devoted themselves to the same task, and saw such fruit from their work that the majority of this small tribe turned to Jesus Christ. One of them, who had himself killed one of the original missionaries, toured England a few years ago with the wife of the man he had killed: both of them not only taught, but demonstrated that the Spirit of Jesus had replaced hatred by love. Love is the greatest thing in the world. We need it badly these days; and the Spirit of Jesus can supply it in unlimited measure. 'God has given us the Holy Spirit to fill our hearts with his love' (Romans 5: 5).

5. A MIND ENLIGHTENED

Fifth, the Spirit of Jesus can renew your mind. My job for the last fifteen years has lain in theological education. I have seen folk who have failed every exam, and been thrown out of school at fifteen, not only equip themselves for the intellectually demanding work of the ordained ministry, but in many cases get a degree as well. If this had occurred once or twice it would have been remarkable. But it happened every year. Once the Spirit of Christ takes over the personality, he opens up all sorts of doors: the mental door is one of them. I believe that the Spirit enlivens our intellectual faculties, enabling us to see truth in a way we had been blind to before. And by this I do not mean merely spiritual truth, as though such a thing existed. All truth is God's truth, and once the Spirit of Truth enters a man's soul, we ought not to be surprised if his capacity for truth and knowledge grows. I think of a colleague of mine on the college staff whom I had taught in earlier days. He had left school at fifteen, entirely unqualified. He found Christ shortly afterwards, and thereafter the growth of his personality, not least on the intellectual side, began. He taught himself up to 'O' and 'A' level standard, gained entry to college, got a good degree, followed it with a M.Th. and a Ph.D., and is now an author, a university teacher, and a minister in the heart of a great university city. That is perhaps the most outstanding example I know of what the Spirit of God is constantly doing: opening blind eyes to the truth. The Spirit of life invariably enlivens our perceptions. St. Augustine found that. He held out long enough against the Spirit of God, but eventually he gave in, and his mind as well as his heart was captivated and renewed by the Spirit of the Lord. It can happen with you. You will not necessarily become an Augustine, but you will find your insight deepened, and your capacity to read, understand, and learn enhanced.

6. A BODY RENEWED

Sixth, the Spirit of Jesus can change your bodily health. I wish to be careful here, because many false claims are made on this score. Instant healing is as suspect as most other 'instant' products of our impatient world. Moreover, it is clear that the Spirit of Jesus does not always heal a man physically. Even in the days of Jesus and the apostles not everyone who came to them with illnesses was healed. In some cases, we are told it was because of their unbelief. Paul himself was not cured of an affliction he called his 'thorn in the flesh', and we read of him

leaving Trophimus at Miletus sick, and Timothy with an un-
healed stomach complaint. Nevertheless he had the power to
heal, and the pages of the Acts, as well as the Epistles, are full
of examples of the healing work of the Spirit of God once he is
allowed into a man's life. And isn't this just what you would
expect? God is the author of all healing, whether 'miraculous'
or through normal medical means. Would it be all that surprising if he undertook major repairs in the body he was beginning to inhabit? After all, the New Testament makes it very
plain that church buildings are not where we are to find the
Holy Spirit, but people themselves: 'Your bodies are the
temples of the Holy Spirit.' All over the world Christians are
waking up to this long-neglected truth, that the Spirit of God
can and does heal, not only non-organic diseases, but organic
ones like cancer and blindness. I have been slow to admit this,
and have even written cautiously against it in a previous book,
but have now met so many people who have been healed once
they opened their lives to the Spirit that I can only bewail my
previous unbelief, and rejoice in the healing work which the
Spirit of God does do in some cases reckoned incurable by the
medical profession.

7. THE CONSCIENCE CLEANSED

Seventh, the Spirit of Jesus can cleanse the conscience. There is
a lovely passage in the Letter to the Hebrews which explains
that the blood of Christ, that is to say his atoning death on the
cross, when applied to the individual by the Holy Spirit, can
cleanse the conscience. Now that is a marvellous thing. One
eminent psychiatrist said that if his mental patients could have
their accusing consciences stilled and be assured of forgiveness,
half of his hospital beds would become empty at once. I think
of a woman I know whose conscience deeply accused her for
sleeping with a married man. She cared a lot about him, and
could not break it; but she knew it was wrong. Then she heard
the good news of Jesus, his love, his pardon, and his ability to
change people's lives. She surrendered her life to him. She

poured out her heart in confession. She was absolutely sure of
his pardon, for 'if we confess our sins, He is faithful and just to
forgive us our sins and to cleanse us from all unrighteousness'.
The Spirit of God not only broke the power of that habit in her
at one fell swoop, but gave her deep assurance in her inner
being that Christ has dealt with her sin, and that her conscience
could no longer condemn her. That woman came with me some
weeks later on a ward round, talking to patients about Jesus.
Her joy, her confidence, and the manifest change in her life
were wonderful to see. The Spirit of God assures us we belong;
he gives an inner witness that God has accepted us into his
family (Romans 8: 16). And that is treasure indeed.

8. SEX LIFE TRANSFORMED

Eighth, the Spirit of Jesus can change your sexual life. This is
an area that requires spring-cleaning in most of us. It did in the
earliest Christians too. Paul is explicit on the point. 'Do not be
deceived,' he says. 'Neither fornicators nor adulterers nor
homosexuals . . . nor drunkards shall enter the kingdom of God.
And such were some of you. But you are washed. You are acquitted. You are set apart for the Lord, through the person of
the Lord Jesus and the Spirit of our God' (1 Corinthians 6: 10,
11). The lives of these immoral folk in Corinth had been transformed by the power of the Spirit entering their lives and set-
ting them free. The same remains true today.

I think of a girl who had turned violently anti-Christian. The
reason, I discovered, was because she had been sleeping with
her boy friend, and found this incompatible with carrying on a
Christian life. She came to rededicate her life, and was willing
to sleep with him no more until they got married. She was,
however, very frightened of how he would react. But such is the
generosity of God that he dealt with her boy friend just as he
had with her. That very weekend forty miles away — and quite
unaware of what had happened to her — he allowed the Spirit
of Christ to take control of his sex life: but he wondered what
his girl friend would say! You can imagine the joy with which

they met, and the new level at which their relationship continued. I still possess a delightful letter from them telling me of the tremendous joy it brought them to surrender their relationship to the Lordship of the Spirit and discover the moral power and the joy in self-discipline which he brought them.

Again, I think of several occasions when a marriage has been on the point of breaking up; and then the Spirit of Christ has been welcomed into the hearts of both partners. The result has been staggering. No longer were they jaded with each other, no longer in search of fresh thrills with other partners. They had discovered a new bond of unity, undergirding the physical, legal and mental unity which threatened to be insufficient to hold them together.

I had a letter not long ago from a homosexual. He had heard the Gospel, rejected it, and had gone to live in a homosexual flat. He had not been able to forget what he had heard about Jesus, however, and set himself to read the New Testament. What he found there, and the testimony of another Christian he came across, brought him to Christ. He surrendered his sexual urges to the Lord, and found that he was able thereafter to have a normal heterosexual relationship. He is now happily married. I do not know whether this is possible in all cases of inversion. Very possibly not. But the Spirit of God which can enable a heterosexually-inclined person to live a pure single life, can also enable a homosexually-inclined person not to indulge his appetites. Of that I am very sure. And the single life is no dead end. It enables you to do many things that a married person cannot do. See what Paul had to say about its advantages in 1 Corinthians 7. And remember that Jesus, the most balanced man who ever lived, remained single — *and fulfilled*! Do not believe the modern myth that nobody can be normal and fulfilled without overt sexual activity. That is a lie. If the Spirit of God calls you to a single life, he will so fulfil and satisfy you that you are thrilled with your lot, and would not choose anything different if you could have your time all over again. Yes, the Spirit can and does make an enormous difference where our sexual drives are concerned.

9. RESCUE FROM DESPAIR

Ninth, the Spirit of Jesus can change your despair. Maybe you haven't got any, but lots of people have these days. Not just despair at the political, industrial and moral chaos of our times, but the much deeper despair of living in a universe which seems to them to be random and purposeless. Jacques Monod put it well in his *Chance and Necessity* when he wrote, 'Our number came up in the Monte Carlo game. Is it surprising that the person who has just made a million at the casino should feel strange and empty?' Or, as Camus put it in his *Caligula*, 'What is intolerable is to see one's life drained of meaning, to be told there is no reason for existing. A man can't live without some reason for living.' The Holy Spirit gives just that reason for living, just that sense of purpose which many of the most perceptive modern men are painfully aware that they lack. The New Testament writers spoke of 'joy in the Holy Spirit', and they showed it in the quality of their lives. They certainly had something to exult about, and so have we. If your Creator sets such value on you that he died to reconcile you to himself and then comes to indwell your very life, that gives fantastic sense of worth and purpose to your very existence. I remember being struck by this a few years ago when reading of the joy of some prisoners in Penang jail who had been brought to faith in Christ by a prison visitor before their execution, and who wrote a letter so remarkable that although I quoted it in *Man Alive* I think it bears repetition. It shows with great clarity the sense of wellbeing, of purpose, of joy which the Spirit of Jesus brings into a life, even if that life faces almost immediate extinction on the human plane.

Our dear Rev. Khoo,
We do thank you from the bottom of our hearts . . . for all you have done for us. You were everything in our hour of need. You were the beacon that guided us to the haven of Jesus Christ. You taught us to have unquestioning faith in God's Word, to pray to him, and to ask for his forgiveness.

During these long agonising months of mental torture . . . till now we stand at the very brink of death, at the very edge of eternity, you have given us so much of yourself in selfless devotion. It is through you that we now look death in the face with courage and calmness, for we doubt not God's promise of forgiveness by the simple act of belief and acceptance. We know that in three and one half hour's time when we pass from off this earth, our Lord and Saviour Jesus Christ will be waiting with open arms to lead us to our new home in the house of the Father . . . With our dying breath we once again affirm to you our undying gratitude — gratitude that will transcend even death itself.

I think of a man I met today. He is a black Rhodesian, a leading member of the Africa National Congress. He had been operating with the freedom fighters in the north of Rhodesia, filled with hate towards the whites, filled with despair about his country's prospects under continued domination of the six million blacks by a quarter of a million whites. But his life had been transformed by the power of Jesus Christ, replacing hatred by love and violence by non-violent (but equally passionate) opposition to oppression. No longer does he think in terms of colour and revenge. He has close friends among the whites who also share his loyalty to Christ. The man is a new creature in the same old skin. He is liberated. He has no trace of a chip on the shoulder, despite having been five times imprisoned and beaten by the Security Forces. He has a clear vision of how his life is to be deployed: in building a new society in Rhodesia, black and white together, in the liberating power of Christ who rescues men from despair.

10. CHARACTER REFINED

Tenth, the Spirit of Jesus can make a new man of you. The pages of the New Testament are full of examples of the transformation the Spirit of Jesus makes to the most unlikely characters once he is invited in. Think of the change in a top

ranking Roman governor like Sergius Paulus. Think of a vacil-
lating cowardly braggart like Simon Peter in the Gospels, who
became the rock man of the early church, fearless in the face of
opposition, sleeping peacefully the night before his execution:
that change was due to the Spirit. Think of a rabid opponent of
Jesus like Saul of Tarsus, converted and changed beyond all
recognition by the Spirit of the one he had once persecuted and
then come to love. Perhaps, though, there is no more remarkable example of the way God's Spirit makes new men of people
than the tiny one-page letter of Paul to Philemon. Philemon
was a rich landowner, converted to Christ through St. Paul's
ministry. He had a slave, Onesimus, who took his opportunity
one day, and ran off with a fair whack of Philemon's cash. By
one of the humorous coincidences that God seems to delight in,
Onesimus landed up in the same prison as Paul! You can guess
what happened next. Paul led the man to Christ, and at once
Onesimus' conscience started to work. Ought he not to go back
to the master he had robbed? Yes, but Philemon would surely
kill him, as owners were in a habit of doing to runaway slaves.
So Paul wrote this little gem of a letter to the Christian landowner about his runaway and now Christian slave. He commends Onesimus not only to Philemon's forgiveness, but also to
his respect as a fellow man and to his love as a fellow Christian.
Now think of the revolution in those two characters, Philemon
and Onesimus. It so happens that we have a papyrus fragment
from roughly this time, coming from a slave owner whose slave
had run away. The writer encourages the recipient to hunt
down the man and kill him. And Philemon forgives his slave,
respects his slave, and loves his slave like a brother! As for
Onesimus, the last thing in the world he would normally do
would be to go back to the landowner from whom he had escaped. Now that he had come to Christ, and was beginning to
be changed by his Spirit, his conscience awoke, and he was
prepared to go back, risk death, offer reparations for what he
had stolen, and live on as a slave in Philemon's employment. As
a matter of fact, reading between the lines of Paul's letter to
Philemon, we find a strong hint that Philemon should release

the man and give him his freedom. I guess he did. And it may be mere coincidence, but we do find that the Christian bishop in that part of the world twenty years later was a man called Onesimus ...

That runaway slave reminds me of a modern half-parallel. I know a man who went into the ordained ministry, but who did not know the life-changing power of the Spirit of Jesus. He laboured away for five years without any results, threw in his hand, and resigned from the ministry. He dropped out of 'straight' society. He became an unemployed thug, slave to women, to drink, and to smoking. He was one of life's casualties. I had the joy of introducing that man to Christ. There was a group who loved and cared for him and sustained him in the early days. He came to train afresh in Britain before going back overseas to the ministry from which he had withdrawn. And God has given him particular gifts as an evangelist among the tough down-and-outs, the drug-takers, the drunks and prostitutes whose scene he knows so well. Needless to say the slavery to drink and tobacco has been snapped, and his whole character gradually transformed.

We may not be slaves and thieves like Onesimus. We may not be in bondage to alcoholism and promiscuity like my friend. But in a sense we are all Onesimuses. We all have habits to which we are enslaved. We have learnt to live with those habits, to be comfortable with them, to excuse them with the refrain, 'Well, you can't change human nature'. To that the Spirit of Jesus replies, 'You must be joking. Changing human nature is my business.'

II

...*To the Reader*

IF YOU HAVE been with me thus far, where does this land us? I began, you will recall, with a plea for honesty; to have done with parrot cries that come so unthinkingly to our lips as we evade the issue of God. We then looked at a series of these common responses about religion. It was clear that we cannot with integrity claim that we are not the religious sort, as if that got us out of looking at the evidence. We went on to examine some of that evidence which made it much harder not to believe in God than to believe in him, whilst recognising that you cannot actually prove personal existence of any kind, your own or God's. It became clear that although there are many true sayings preserved in many religions and many impressive lives lived by their practitioners, it is neither logical nor possible to suppose that all religions lead to God. Indeed, there is more than a streak in human nature which does not want to know too much about God and is very keen to profess agnosticism about his existence, or at least to keep him at a distance: his closer presence would be altogether too demanding and uncomfortable. But his closer presence is just what we seem to have to face. Jesus confronts us with it. And it simply will not do to class Jesus Christ among the great prophets or the good men of the world. The old dilemma remains: he is either God or he is not good. No 'good man' made the claims he did. No 'good man' rose from the dead.

If, in Jesus, God himself has come to look for us, it clearly will not do to imagine that so long as we are sincere, it does not matter what we believe. Nor will doing our best solve our problems. Our best is manifestly not good enough for ourselves, let alone God. Even if we could keep the Ten Commandments and the Sermon on the Mount for the rest of our days, that would not alter the past, or erase its ugly blots. The more I know people, the more certain I am of the truth of the Bible's diagnosis: 'The heart of a man is deceitful above all things, and desperately wicked.' Everybody has a past which contains things of which he has good reason to be ashamed. And nothing can alter the past: nothing, that is, if we leave out of account the death of Jesus to put sinful people like us in the clear with God. Had there been any other way, we can be sure God would have taken it, rather than allow Jesus to go to that grim cross. The cross, then, is very much the heart of Christianity; ours is a faith which has a gallows as its badge. On that gallows the most important battle of history was fought and won: Christ there suffered for sins, the righteous one for the unrighteous, to bring us to God.

Nor was that all. Christians do not remember with gratitude a dead Christ. They rejoice in the companionship of a living Lord who rose from the grave and lives today. This resurrection is as crucial to Christianity as is the cross. It means that there is a life after death. It means that Jesus can bring us there. It means his atoning death was sufficient to deal with a world's sin. It means his conquering presence is available to battle on against ingrained evil in his people. And this is where the Holy Spirit comes in. For, as we saw in the last chapter, the Spirit can be described as Jesus' 'other self', the one who makes him real to believing people all over the world, and who works out in them the character of Jesus.

Such is God's provision for us, when really we had no claim on him at all. His generosity is breathtaking. What is to be done about it? May I make some simple suggestions?

RESPONSE

Reflect on this amazing fact, that he did this not just for the world or for the next man, but for *you*. He loves you. He made you. He died for you. He waits to come and live in your life. You need his spring-cleaning. You need his pardon, his guidance, his joy, his sticking power, his courage in the face of death. These qualities are available to you, but only in Jesus Christ.

Is this, perhaps, the moment to kneel down and make your personal response to the love of God? 'The gift of God is eternal life,' says the New Testament. What do you do with a gift? You accept it gratefully. It is just the same with Jesus. He is God's great gift to you: all the other gifts are wrapped up in him. Do not duck the issue by waiting till you're good enough: you never will be. Just accept the gift thankfully, perhaps in words like these:

Lord, I am amazed at your generosity. I don't deserve it. I can hardly believe it. But I do dimly feel you are there, and I realise that you came to this earth for me in Jesus Christ. I do believe he died for my sins and is alive so that he can come by his Spirit into my heart. I realise that he wants to involve me in his ongoing work and among his people, and I am prepared for that. Lord, here and now I accept in faith the gift of Jesus to me personally. Please never allow me to go back on this decision, and please enable me to live worthy of it in your strength, wherever future circumstances take me.

PROSPECT

Having taken this momentous step, tell someone about it. Write to me if you don't know anyone who would be sympathetic. But better, tell a Christian friend or relative. They will be thrilled and encouraged. Maybe they have been praying for you for some time — someone (a mother, a friend, a colleague) nearly always has when a person makes a definite commitment to Christ. To tell someone else is important for two reasons. One, it puts you into contact with others who can help you on in the early days of your discipleship. Two, it enables you to nail your colours to the mast: and the New Testament is insistent on the need for this. 'If you confess with your mouth the Lord Jesus, and believe in your heart that God raised him from the dead, you will be saved.' Of course, this will involve in due course 'letting your light so shine before men that they may see your good works and glorify your Father who is in heaven'. But it may be as well to start with Christians first, before going to tell the toughest atheist you know that you have surrendered your life to Jesus Christ! At all events, open, unashamed discipleship is called for. Secret disciples never grow.

Next, it would be a good idea to read something on the basic essentials in Christian living, so as to have, as it were, a bird's eye view of what it will involve. If you have almost no time, read J. R. W. Stott's booklet *Being a Christian* (Inter Varsity Press). If you have a bit more time, read David Watson's *Live a New Life* (Inter Varsity Press), or my own recent *New Life New Lifestyle* (Hodder & Stoughton). In this way you will quickly get some ideas about going on in the companionship of the one you have begun to trust.

Third, it is most important to get involved in Christian fellowship. The church, for all its failings, is not a luxury but a necessity. Jesus did not just come to save individuals but to set up on earth a first instalment of the Kingdom of God. And that means a society. You cannot get away from it. From now on your lot is cast with the Christian church. Where it is corrupt, purge it. Where it is slack, enliven it. Where it is right, follow it. But join it you must. So if you are not baptised, it is high time to seek out a minister in some lively church who will prepare you for baptism. If your denomination baptises infants, you may well already be baptised. In that case, you will want to get confirmed, or the equivalent way of entry into full membership, so that you can pull your weight in the local congregation, take part in the Holy Communion, and give public testimony to your allegiance to Christ.

Next, may I pass on a piece of advice which I found invaluable in the early days of following Christ? Is there some Christian friend whom you know well? If so, he will be able to help you a great deal if you meet him regularly, not only socially but in order to read a bit of the Bible together, to talk over any difficulties as they occur, and to learn from him how to engage in real prayer (as opposed to the bedside noises you may have uttered for a long time without developing them at all). I had, for some months, a weekly session with such a friend, and it made all the difference.

Finally, get involved in some piece of Christian service. It does not much matter what it is so long as you do it for Jesus' sake and to help other people. Pray to be guided to the contribution you could best make. But get stuck in. Don't be a drone in the Christian hive, sucking up the honey and doing none of the work. Christian service is one of the great ways of growing to maturity in the Christian life.

Well, there it is. That would be the author's hope for his readers. I am sure that if you commit yourself realistically and wholeheartedly to God in this way you will cease to produce the parrot cries that may have satisfied you up till now ('All religions lead to God', 'It doesn't matter what you believe so long as you are sincere' and the rest). Instead you will begin to produce the cries of the newly born child of God as the Spirit gets to work within you, enabling you to cry, 'Abba, dear Father'.

Further Reading

for those who wish to examine some issues in greater depth.

ABOUT GOD

Knowing God, James Packer (Hodder & Stoughton)
The Living God, Dick France (I.V.P.)
The God Who is There, Francis Schaeffer (Hodder & Stoughton)
Does God exist? A. E. Taylor (Fontana)

ABOUT ALTERNATIVES TO CHRISTIAN BELIEF

The Dust of Death, Os Guinness (I.V.P.)
Christian Faith and Other Faiths, Stephen Neill (O.U.P.)
The Finality of Christ, Lesslie Newbiggin (S.C.M.)
Christianity and Comparative Religion, J. N. D. Anderson (I.V.P.)

ABOUT SUFFERING

The Problem of Pain, C. S. Lewis (Fontana)
A Grief Observed, C. S. Lewis (Fontana)
Why do Men Suffer? L. Weatherhead (S.C.M.)
Taught by Pain, ed. Mary Endersbee (Falcon)

ABOUT MAN'S NATURE

I Believe in Man, George Carey (Hodder & Stoughton, publishing 1977)
What is Human? T. M. Kitwood (I.V.P.)

ABOUT SCIENCE

Beyond Science, Denis Alexander (Lion)
World without End, Roger Pilkington (Macmillan)
Adam and the Ape, R. J. Berry (Falcon)
Science and Christian Belief, C. A. Coulson (S.C.M.)
The Clockwork Image, D. M. Mackay (I.V.P.)

ABOUT PHILOSOPHY

Faith Facing Facts, R. N. Williams (Coverdale)
Teach Yourself Philosophy of Religion, H. D. Lewis
    (Hodder & Stoughton)
Philosophy and the Christian Faith, Colin Brown (Tyndale)

ABOUT CHRISTIAN EVIDENCES

Runaway World, Michael Green (I.V.P.)
Mere Christianity, C. S. Lewis (Fontana)
My God is Real, D. C. K. Watson (Falcon)
Christianity on Trial, Colin Chapman (Lion)

ABOUT JESUS

The Gospels — in a modern translation
The Founder of Christianity, C. H. Dodd (Fontana)
Meet Jesus, Geoff Treasure (Falcon)

ABOUT THE RESURRECTION

I Believe in the Resurrection of Jesus, George Ladd (Hodder
    & Stoughton)
First Easter, Paul Maier (Mowbrays)
Man Alive, Michael Green (I.V.P.)

ABOUT THE CROSS

Why the Cross? H. E. Guillebaud (I.V.P.)
The Cross in the New Testament, L. Morris (Paternoster)
The Death of Christ, James Denney (Tyndale)

ABOUT THE HOLY SPIRIT

Reflected Glory, Thomas Smail (Hodder & Stoughton)
I Believe in the Holy Spirit, Michael Green (Hodder & Stoughton)
The Go Between God, J. V. Taylor (S.C.M.)

BIBLE READING AIDS

The Scripture Union Notes,
The Soldier's Armoury (Hodder & Stoughton)
Every day with Jesus (Christian Literature Crusade)
The Bible Reading Fellowship

PRAYER

The Prayers of the New Testament, Donald Coggan (Hodder & Stoughton)
Prayers of Life, Michel Quoist (Gill)
How to Talk with God, Stephen Winward (Hodder & Stoughton)
Our Understanding of Prayer, I. T. Ramsey (S.P.C.K.)
Prayer, O. Hallesby (I.V.P.)
The Use of Praying, J. Neville Ward (Epwarth)